ISBN 978-0-243-20754-1
PIBN 10788931

1 MONTH OF
FREE
READING

at
www.ForgottenBooks.com

English
Français
Deutsche
Italiano
Español
Português

www.forgottenbooks.com

Mythology Photography **Fiction**
Fishing Christianity **Art** Cooking
Essays Buddhism Freemasonry
Medicine **Biology** Music **Ancient**
Egypt Evolution Carpentry Physics
Dance Geology **Mathematics** Fitness
Shakespeare **Folklore** Yoga Marketing
Confidence Immortality Biographies
Poetry **Psychology** Witchcraft
Electronics Chemistry History **Law**
Accounting **Philosophy** Anthropology
Alchemy Drama Quantum Mechanics
Atheism Sexual Health **Ancient History**
Entrepreneurship Languages Sport
Paleontology Needlework Islam
Metaphysics Investment Archaeology
Parenting Statistics Criminology
Motivational

THE NEW

SCOTTISH PSALTER

BEING THE

BOOK OF PSALMS

MARKED FOR EXPRESSIVE SINGING

WITH

TUNES CONTAINED IN "CHURCH MELODIES"

BY THE

In intro ucing t s   ,   g   j
ourselves of the following extracts from Calvin's preface to the *Genevan Psalter*.*

To all Christians, lovers of the Word of God, greeting

As it is a thing enjoined in christianity, and amongst the most necessary, that every believer, in his own place, should observe and maintain the communion of the church, frequenting the assemblies which are held on Sabbaths and other days, to honour and serve God; so it is right and reasonable, that all should know and understand what is said and done in the place of worship, so as to draw from it advantage and edification. For our Lord has not instituted the order which we are to observe, when we meet in his name, to amuse the world as a spectacle—but rather has desired, that everything should redound to the profit of all his people, as Saint Paul witnesseth, commanding that everything that is done in the church, should have regard to the common edification of all, which the servant (Paul) would not have enjoined had it not been the design of the Master. But that cannot be done, unless we are so instructed as to understand everything which has been ordained for our good. For to say that we can have devotion, whether in prayers, or ceremonies, without understanding anything of them, is a great mockery, however commonly this is said.

A good affection towards God is not a dead and passive thing, but it is a lively emotion proceeding from the Holy Spirit, when the heart is rightly touched, and the understanding enlightened; and truly if one could be edified by things which one sees without knowing what they mean, Saint Paul would not have so rigorously forbidden to speak in an unknown tongue, and would not have used the argument that there is no edification, where there is no doctrine. Therefore if we wish duly to honour the holy ordinances of our Lord, which we observe in the church, the chief thing is to know what they mean, and are designed to express, and to what object they tend, in order that the observance of them may be useful and salutary, and consequently rightly regulated.

    .   .   .   .

As for public prayers, there are two kinds of them—the one is expressed in words only, the other with song; and this is no recent invention, for from the first origin of the church, this has been the case, bridle of dissoluteness, that it should not lead to voluptuousness, nor be the instrument of immodesty and impurity.

But further, there is scarcely anything in this world which can more powerfully turn or bend hither and thither the manners of men, as Plato has wisely remarked. And in fact we experimentally feel that it has a secret and incredible power over our hearts to move them one way or other. Therefore we ought to be so much the more careful to regulate it in such a manner, that it may be useful to us, and in no ways pernicious. For this reason, the ancient doctors of the church often complained that the people of their time were addicted to disgraceful and immodest songs, which, not without cause, they esteemed and called a deadly and satanic poison for corrupting the world.

But in speaking of music I include two parts, to wit, the words, or subject and matter; secondly, the song or melody. It is true that all evil words, as saith St. Paul, corrupt good manners, but when melody is united to them, they much more powerfully pierce the heart, and enter in: just as when by a funnel wine is poured into a vessel, so poison and corruption is infused into the depth of the heart by the melody.

What then is to be done? It is to have songs not only pure, but also holy, that they may be incitements to stir us up to pray to and praise God, and to meditate on His works, in order to love Him, fear Him, honour and glorify Him. But what Saint Augustine says is true, that none can sing things worthy of God but he who has received the power from Himself. Wherefore when we have sought all round, searching here and there, we shall find no songs better and more suitable for this end than the Psalms of David which the Holy Spirit dictated and gave to him. And therefore when we sing them, we are as certain that God has put words into our mouths as if He Himself sang within us to exalt His glory. Wherefore Chrysostom exhorts all men and women and little children to accustom themselves to sing them as a means of associating themselves with the company of angels; further, we must remember what St. Paul says, that spiritual songs cannot be sung well but with the heart; but the heart requires the understanding: and in that saith St. Augustine lies the difference between the song of man and that of birds, for a linnet, a nightingale, and a jay *(papegay)*, may sing well, but it will be without understanding.

But the peculiar gift of man is to sing knowing what he says. Further, the understanding ought to accompany the heart and affections, which cannot be unless we have the song imprinted in our memory, that we may be ever singing it.

This present book, for this cause, besides what otherwise has been said, ought to be particularly acceptable to every one who desires, without reproach, and according to God, to rejoice in seeing his own salvation, and the good of his neighbours; and thus has no need to be much recommended by me, as it carries in itself its own value and praise. Only let the world be well advised, that instead of songs partly vain and frivolous, partly foolish and dull, partly filthy and vile, and consequently wicked and hurtful, which it has heretofore used, it should accustom itself hereafter to sing these heavenly and divine songs, with good king David.

Touching the music, it appeared best that it should be simple in the way we have put it, to carry weight and majesty suitable to the subject, and even to be fit to be sung in church as has been said.

GENEVA, 10th June 1543.

To these words so fitly spoken, it is scarcely necessary to add anything. It is hoped that the addition of expression marks on the margin will not unduly distract the attention, while it may assist the worshipper in seizing the sentiment of the psalm. Imperfections may, doubtless, be found in the execution of the idea; but those who are best acquainted with the difficulties will be the most ready to excuse them.

THE

PSALMS OF DAVID

IN METRE.

NOTE.

An attempt is made in this New Psalter to mark the words more fully than has hitherto been attempted, for Expressive Singing.   In addition to the use of *italics* for the softer passages, and CAPITALS for the stronger, the ordinary musical signs of expression have also been employed. These have been printed in the margin, and are the following ·—

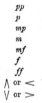

pp
p
mp
m
mf
f
ff
∧ or <
∨ or >

Where the prevailing character of a psalm is soft, it has not been thought necessary to make a large use of italics; nor when bold, of capitals.

It is hoped that the book may afford some help to singing the Songs of Sion with the spirit and with the understanding.

THE PSALMS OF DAVID

IN METRE:

ACCORDING TO

THE VERSION APPROVED BY THE CHURCH OF SCOTLAND, AND APPOINTED
TO BE USED IN WORSHIP.

PRINTED BY AUTHORITY.

PAISLEY: J. AND R. PARLANE, 97 HIGH STREET.

LICENSE.

In terms of Her Majesty's Letters Patent to Her Printers for Scotland, and of the Instructions issued by Her Majesty in Council, dated Eleventh July one thousand eight hundred and thirty nine, I hereby license and authorise James and Robert Farlane, Printers, Paisley, to print within the premises situated in Number Eight School Wynd, Paisley, and to publish, as by the authority of Her Majesty, an Edition of the Psalms of David in Metre, in long primer type, foolscap octavo size, consisting of Three thousand copies, as proposed in their Declaration, dated Twenty Second December, one thousand eight hundred and sixty nine, the terms and conditions of the said instructions being always, and in all points fully complied with and observed by the said James and Robert Parlane

G. YOUNG.

Edinburgh, 29th December 1869.

THE PSALMS OF DAVID

IN METRE.

PSALM I.

Abbey 56.   Jackson's 51.

m 1 THAT man hath perfect blessedness
     who walketh not astray
  In counsel of ungodly men,
     nor stands in sinners' way,
  Nor sitteth in the scorner's chair:
  2   But placeth his delight
  Upon God's law, and meditates
     on his law day and night.

mf 3 He shall be like a tree that grows
     near planted by a river,

his fruit,
:

m

f

PSALM II.

Montrose 49.   Bedford 61.

mf 1 WHY rage the heathen? and vain things
     why do the people mind?

m 2 Kings of the earth do set themselves,
     and princes are combin'd,
To plot against the Lord, and his
     Anointed, saying thus,

3 Let us asunder break their bands,
     and cast their cords from us.

ff 4 HE THAT IN HEAVEN SITS SHALL LAUGH;
     THE LORD SHALL SCORN THEM ALL.

5 THEN SHALL HE SPEAK TO THEM IN WRATH,
     IN RAGE HE VEX THEM SHALL.

mf 6 Yet, notwithstanding, I have him
     to be my King appointed;
And over Sion, my holy hill,
     I have him King anointed.

7 The sure decree I will declare·
     the Lord hath said to me,
Thou art mine only Son; this day
     I have begotten thee.

8

f 9

∧

m 10

mp 11

12

∧

m

:

PSALM III.

Gloucester 54.   Coleshill 146.

pp 1 O LORD, *how are my foes increas'd!*
     against me many rise.

2 *Many say of my soul, For him*
   in God no succour lies.

f 3 YET THOU MY SHIELD AND GLORY ART,
   TH' UPLIFTER OF MINE HEAD.

m 4 I cry'd, and, from his holy hill,
   the Lord me answer made.

p 5 I laid me down and slept, I wak'd;   *mf* 3
   for God sustained me.

  6 I WILL NOT FEAR THOUGH THOUSANDS TEN
   SET ROUND AGAINST ME BE.

mp 7 Arise, O Lord; save me, my God;
   for thou my foes hast stroke
   All on the cheek-bone, and the teeth   *mf* 5
   of wicked men hast broke.

f 8 SALVATION DOTH APPERTAIN   *mp* 6
   UNTO THE LORD ALONE:
   THY BLESSING, LORD, FOR EVERMORE   *mf*
   THY PEOPLE IS UPON.

PSALM IV.

Martyrdom 64. *Ver.* 1-5 *Abbey* 56. *Ver.* 6-8 *St. Gregory* 73

mp 1 GIVE ear unto me when I call,
   God of my righteousness:

p 8 *I will both lay me down in peace,*
    and quiet sleep will take;
    Because thou only me to dwell
    in safety, Lord, dost make.

PSALM V.

Denfield 124.   *Morven* 99.

m 8

mp 1 GIVE ear unto my words, O Lord,
    my meditation weigh.
  2 Hear my loud cry, my King, my God;
    for I to thee will pray.
m 3 Lord, thou shalt early hear my voice:
    I early will direct
    My pray'r to thee; and, looking up,
    an answer will expect.

p 10

  4 For thou art not a God that doth
    in wickedness delight;
    Neither shall evil dwell with thee,
  5   Nor fools stand in thy sight.
    All that ill-doers are thou hat'st;
  6   Cutt'st off that liars be:

f 11

m 12 For, Lord, unto the righteous man
    thou wilt thy blessing yield :
    With favour thou wilt compass him
    about, as with a shield.

PSALM VI.

Babylon Streams 29.   Luther's Prayer 199.

p 1 LORD, in thy wrath rebuke me not ;
    Nor in thy hot rage chasten me.
pp 2 *Lord, pity me, for I am weak:*
    Heal me, for my bones vexed be.
  3 *My soul is also vexed sore ;*
m   But, Lord, how long stay wilt thou make?
  4 Return, O Lord, my soul set free ;
    O SAVE ME, for thy mercies' sake.

pp 5 *Because those that deceased are*
    Of thee shall no remembrance have ;
    And who is he that will to thee
    Give praises lying in the grave?
p 6 I with my groaning weary am,
    I also all the night my bed

Have caused for to swim ; and I
With tears my couch have watered.

10

Another of the same.

Silesia 149   *Dundee* 144

p

pp

:

3 *My soul is vexed sore:* but, Lord,
  how long stay wilt thou make?
∧ 4 Return, Lord, free my soul; and save
  me, for thy mercies' sake.   10
pp 5 *Because of thee in death there shall*
  no more remembrance be:
  Of those that in the grave do lie,
  who shall give thanks to thee?

p 6 I with my groaning weary am,
  and all the night my bed
  I caused for to swim; with tears   m 1
  my couch I watered.
7 By reason of my vexing grief
  mine eye consumed is·
  It waxeth old, because of all   p 2
  that be mine enemies.

m 8 But now, depart from me, all ye   ◊
  that work iniquity:
  For why? the Lord hath heard my voice,   m 3
  when I did mourn and cry.
9 Unto my supplication
  the Lord did hearing give:

PSALM VII.

St. Neot 150   *St. Nicholas* 151

I

:

PSALM VII

/\   4 If I rewarded ill to him
         that was at peace with me;
         (Yea, ev'n the man that without cause   _mf_ 10
          my foe was I did free;)
_f_   5 THEN LET THE FOE PURSUE AND TAKE   11
         MY SOUL, AND MY LIFE THRUST
         Down TO THE EARTH, and let him lay   _m_ 12
\/   mine honour in the dust.
_m_   6 Rise in thy wrath, Lord, raise thyself,
         for my foes raging be;
         And, to the judgment which thou hast   13
          commanded, wake for me.
      7 So shall th' assembly of thy folk
         about encompass thee:
         Thou therefore, for their sakes, return   14
          unto thy place on high.
      8 The Lord he shall the people judge:
         my judge, JEHOVAH, be,
         After my righteousness, and mine   15
          integrity in me.

      9 O let the wicked's malice end;
         but stablish stedfastly

;

9. Angels' Hymn. L.M.

♩ = 72

DR. O. GIBBONS, 1623.

Who can de - scribe the joys that rise Through all the courts of par - a - dise,

To see a pro - di - gal re - turn, To see an heir of glo - ry born.

2 In thee, most High, I'll greatly joy,
  and sing unto thy name.

mf 3 When back my foes were turn'd, they fell,
  and perish'd at thy sight :

4 For thou maintain'dst my right and cause;
  on throne sat'st judging right.

mp 5 The heathen thou rebuked hast
  the wicked overthrown ;

p   *Thou hast put out their names, that they*
  may never more be known.

m 6 O en'my ! now destructions have
  an end perpetual :
  Thou cities raz'd, perish'd with them
  is their memorial.

f 7 God shall endure for aye ; he doth
  for judgment set his throne ;

8 In righteousness to judge the world
  justice to give each one.

m 9 God also will a refuge be
  for those that are oppress'd ;
  A refuge will he be in times
  of trouble to distress'd.

   10

f. 11

mp 12

p 13

m 14

mp 15

And in the net which they have hid
their own feet fast are snar'd.

p 16 The Lord is by the judgment known
which he himself hath wrought:
The sinners' hands do make the snares
wherewith themselves are caught.

17 They who are wicked into hell
each one shall turned be;
And all the nations that forget
to seek the Lord most high.

m 18 For they that needy are shall not
forgotten be alway;
The expectation of the poor
shall not be lost for aye.

∧ 19 Arise, Lord, let not man prevail;
judge heathen in thy sight

∨ 20 That they may know themselves but
the nations, Lord, affright.   [men,

PSALM X.

Ver. 1-11 Crowle 153.   Ver. 12-18 St. Nicho'as 151

p 1 WHEREFORE is it that thou, O
∧   dost stand from us afar ? [Lord,

∨

m 2   r:

3

                    w

4

5

ffeth

6

7 His mouth with cursing, fraud, deceit,
  is fill'd abundantly;
And underneath his tongue there is   13
  mischief and vanity.
8 He closely sits in villages;   *m*
  he slays the innocent:
Against the poor that pass him by   14
  his cruel eyes are bent.

9 He, lion-like, lurks in his den·
  he waits the poor to·take;
And when he draws him in his net   15
  his prey he doth him make.
10 Himself he humbleth very low,
  he croucheth down withal,
That so a multitude of poor   *f* 16
  may by his strong ones fall.

11 He thus hath said within his heart
  The Lord hath quite forgot·
He hides his countenance, and he   *m* 17
  for ever sees it not.
*mf*12 O Lord, do thou arise; O God
  lift up thine hand on high:

18 To judge the fatherless, and those
    that are oppressed sore;
V That man, that is but sprung of earth   *p* 6
    may them oppress no more.

          furious
        :   [*storms,*

PSALM XI.

Coleshill 146. *St Nicholas* 151.   *m* 7

mp 1 I IN the Lord do put my trust;
mf   how is it then that ye
    Say to my soul, Flee, as a bird,
    unto your mountain high?
m 2 For, lo, the wicked bend their bow,   *mp* 1
    their shafts on string they fit
    That those who upright are in heart
    they privily may hit.

  3 If the foundations be destroy'd,   2
    what hath the righteous done?
           :
  4 God in his holy temple is,
    in heaven is his throne: an
    His eyes do see, his eyelids try   *m* 3
  5 men's sons. The just he proves:

4 We'll with our tongue prevail, our lips
   are ours: who's lord o'er us?

mf 5 For poor oppress'd, and for the sighs
   of needy, rise will I,
   Saith God, and him in safety set·
   from such as him defy.

m 6 The words of God are words most pure;
   they be like silver try'd
   In earthen furnace, seven times
   that hath been purify'd.

7 Lord, thou shalt them preserve and keep
   for ever from this race.

8 On each side walk the wicked, when
   vile men are high in place.

PSALM XIII.
Martyrdom 64.   Morven 99.

p 1 HOW long wilt thou forget me, Lord?
   shall it for ever be?
   O how long shall it be that thou
   wilt hide thy face from me?

2 How long take counsel in my soul,
   still sad in heart, shall I?

m 3
f

m 4

f 5

6

mp 1

    They are corrupt, their works are vile;
      not one of them doth good.

2 Upon men's sons the Lord from heav'n   *mp*
    did cast his eyes abroad,
    To see if any understood,
      and did seek after God.

3 They altogether filthy are,
    they all aside are gone;
  ·And there is none that doeth good,
    yea, sure there is not one.

m 4 These workers of iniquity
    do they not know at all,
   That they my people eat as bread,
    and on God do not call?

5 There fear'd they much; for God is with   4
    the whole race of the just.
6 You shame the counsel of the poor,
    because God is his trust.

mf 7 Let Isr'el's help from Sion come:
    when back the Lord shall bring
   His captives, JACOB SHALL REJOICE,
    AND ISRAEL SHALL SING.

PSALM XVI.

Old 137th 35.   Ver. 1-6 Bristol 133.   Ver. 7-11 Tallis 93.

m 1 LORD, keep me; for I trust in thee.
   2 To God thus was my speech,
     Thou art my Lord; and unto thee
     my goodness doth not reach:
   3 To saints on earth, to th' excellent
     where my delight's all plac'd.
mp 4 Their sorrows shall be multiply'd
     to other gods that haste:

m   Of their drink-offerings of blood
     I will no off'ring make;
     Yea, neither I their very names
     up in my lips will take.
f 5 GOD IS OF MINE INHERITANCE
     AND CUP THE PORTION
     THE LOT THAT FALLEN IS TO ME
     THOU DOST MAINTAIN ALONE.

m 6 Unto me happily the lines
     in pleasant places fell;

7

m 8

f 9

m 10

11

f

PSALM XVII.

Farrant 58.   Moravia 87.

mf 1 LORD, hear the right, attend my cry,
        unto my pray'r give heed

m   That doth not in hypocrisy
        from feigned lips proceed.

  2 And from before thy presence forth
        my sentence do thou send:
     Toward these things that equal are
        do thou thine eyes intend.

mp 3 Thou prov'dst mine heart, thou visit'dst
        by night, thou didst me try,   [me
     Yet nothing found'st; for that my mouth
        shall not sin, purpos'd I.

  4 As for men's works, I, by the word
        that from thy lips doth flow,
     Did me preserve out of the paths
        wherein destroyers go.

m 5 Hold up my goings, Lord, me guide
        in those thy paths divine,
     So that my footsteps may not slide
        out of those ways of thine.

6

7

p 8
mp

9

10

11

12

mf 13

those

My soul save from the wicked man,
 the man which is thy sword.
m 14 From men, which are thy hand, O Lord,
 from worldly men me save,
Which only in this present life   m 3
 their part and portion have.

Whose belly with thy treasure hid
 thou fill'st: they children have
In plenty; of their goods the rest   p 4
 they to their children leave.
mf 15 But as for me, I thine own face   5
 in righteousness will see;
And with thy likeness, when I wake   6
 I satisfy'd shall be.

            mf

PSALM XVIII.

Ver. 1-6 St. Nicholas 151, St. Stephen 62. Ver. 7-15 Montrose 49, Old 44th 32. Ver. 16-50 Chingford 91, Colchester 111.

mf 1 THEE will I love, O Lord, my strength.   7
 2   My fortress is the Lord
My rock, and he that doth to me   m 8
 deliverance afford:

Devouring fire, and coals by it
   were turned into flame.   *mf* 14

9 He also bowed down the heav'ns,
   and thence he did descend;
And thickest clouds of darkness did   15
   under his feet attend.

m 10 And he upon a cherub rode,
   and thereon he did fly;
Yea, on the swift wings of the wind   *m* 16
   his flight was from on high.
*mp*11 He darkness made his secret place:
   about him, for his tent,
Dark waters were, and thickest clouds   17
   of th' airy firmament.

m 12 And at the brightness of that light,
   which was before his eye,
His thick clouds pass'd away, hailstones   *p* 18
   and coals of fire did fly.
13 The Lord God also in the heav'ns
ff   DID THUNDER IN HIS IRE;
AND THERE THE HIGHEST GAVE HIS VOICE,   *mf* 19
   HAILSTONES AND COALS OF FIRE.

Because he took delight in me
  he my deliv'rance wrought.

27   in

m 20 According to my righteousness
    he did me recompense,
He me repaid according to
  my hands' pure innocence.

⋀28

21 For I God's ways kept, from my God
    did not turn wickedly.

m

22 His judgments were before me, I
    his laws put not from me.

f 29   I

mp 23 Sincere before him was my heart,
    with him upright was I;
And watchfully I kept myself
  from mine iniquity.

m 30

m 24 After my righteousness the Lord
    hath recompensed me,
After the cleanness of my hands
  appearing in his eye.

⋀
31   he

25 Thou gracious to the gracious art
    to upright men upright

f 32   WITH

26 Pure to the pure, froward thou kyth'st
    unto the froward wight.

mf 33 He made my feet swift as the hinds,
　　　set me on my high places.

34 Mine hands to war he taught, mine arms　　*mp* 41
　　brake bows of steel in pieces.

35 The shield of thy salvation
　　thou didst on me bestow:
　　Thy right hand held me up, and great　　*mf* 42
　　thy kindness made me grow.

36 And in my way my steps thou hast
　　enlarged under me,
　　That I go safely, and my feet　　　　43
　　are kept from sliding free.

37 Mine en'mies I pursued have
　　and did them overtake;
　　Nor did I turn again till I　　　　　44
　　an end of them did make.

38 I wounded them, they could not rise;　45
　　they at my feet did fall.

39 Thou girdedst me with strength for war;　*f* 46
　　my foes thou brought'st down all:

40 And thou hast giv'n to me the necks　　47
　　of all mine enemies;

mf 48 He saves me from mine enemies;   3
    yea, thou hast lifted me
    Above my foes; and from the man   4
    of vi'lence set me free.

f 49 THEREFORE TO THEE WILL I GIVE
        THANKS   5
    THE HEATHEN FOLK AMONG;
    AND TO THY NAME, O LORD, I WILL
      SING PRAISES IN A SONG.   6
mf 50 He great deliv'rance gives his king:
    he mercy doth extend
    To David, his anointed one
    and his seed without end.   *mp* 7

PSALM XIX.

Ver. 1-6 *Liverpool* 69.   *Stroudwater* 74.   8
Ver. 7-14 *Moravia* 87.   *Abbey* 56.

m 1 THE heav'ns God's glory do declare,
    the skies his hand-works preach:
  2 Day utters speech to day, and night   9
    to night doth knowledge teach.

21. Creation. D.L.M.

mp 7 In chariots some put confidence,
     some horses trust upon:
f   BUT WE REMEMBER WILL THE NAME   4
     OF OUR LORD GOD ALONE.

8 We rise, and upright stand, when they
     are bowed down, and fall.
9 Deliver, Lord; and let the King   5
     us hear, when we do call.

PSALM XXI.

Ver. 1-7 Durham 95. Belgrave 110.   6
Ver. 8-13 St. Paul 50. Stafford 94.

mf 1 THE king in thy great strength, O   *mf*
     shall very joyful be: [Lord,
In thy salvation rejoice   *m* 7
     how veh'mently shall he!
m 2 Thou hast bestowed upon him   *mf*
     all that his heart would have;
And thou from him didst not withhold   *m* 8
     whate'er his lips did crave.

3 For thou with blessings him prevent'st
     of goodness manifold: of

9 Like fiery ov'n thou shalt them make,
    when kindled is thine ire;
God shall them swallow in his wrath,   2
    devour them shall the fire.
10 Their fruit from earth thou shalt
    their seed men from among:[destroy,
11 For they beyond their might 'gainst   *m* 3
    did plot mischief and wrong. [thee

12 Thou therefore shalt make them turn   4
    when thou thy shafts shalt place[ack,
Upon thy strings, made ready all b   *m* 5
    to fly against their face.   [Lord,
f 13 In thy great power and strength, O
    be thou exalted high;   [HEARTS,
  So SHALL WE SING WITH JOYFUL
  THY POWER PRAISE SHALL WE.   *pp* 6

PSALM XXII.

Ver. 1-21 *Dundee* 144.   *Crowle* 153.
Ver. 22-26 *Colchester* 111.   *Bedford* 61.
Ver. 27-30 *Durham* 95.   *Sheffield* 105.

pp 1 *MY God, my God, why hast thou me*
    forsaken? why so far   7

m 8 This man did trust in God, that he
　　　would free him by his might:
　　　Let him deliver him, sith he
　　　had in him such delight.
p 9 But thou art he out of the womb
　　　that didst me safely take;
　　　When I was on my mother's breasts
　　　thou me to hope didst make.

10 And I was cast upon thy care,
　　　ev'n from the womb till now;
　　　And from my mother's belly, Lord
　　　my God and guide art thou.
11 Be not far off, for grief is near
　　　and none to help is found.
mp 12 Bulls many compass me, strong bulls
　　　of Bashan me surround.

13 Their mouths they open'd wide on me,
　　　upon me gape did they,
　　　Like to a lion ravening
　　　and roaring for his prey.
pp 14 *Like water I'm pour'd out, my bones*
　　　all out of joint do part:

p 15

p 16

17

18

mp 19

20

21

24. **Ambrose.** L.M.

The bil-lows swell, the winds are high, Clouds o - ver-cast my win-try sky;
Out of the depths to thee I call, My fears are great, my strength is small.

	In pastures green: he leadeth me		*mf*	1
	the quiet waters by.			
m	3 My soul he doth restore again;			
	and me to walk doth make			
	Within the paths of righteousness		*m*	2
	ev'n for his own name's sake.			

pp 4 *Yea, though I walk in death's dark vale,*
m ∧   *yet will I fear none ill :*
  ∨   For thou art with me; and thy rod   *mp* 3
      and staff me comfort still.
mf 5 My table thou hast furnished
      in presence of my foes
      My head thou dost with oil anoint,   *m* 4
      and my cup overflows.   [pure,

    6 Goodness and mercy all my life
      shall surely follow me ·
 ∧   AND IN GOD'S HOUSE FOR EVERMORE   *mf* 5
      MY DWELLING-PLACE SHALL BE.
                                                      ∧   God

PSALM XXIV.

Ver. 1-6 Harrington 120. St. Gregory 73.
Ver. 7-10 St. George's Edin. 38. Vienna 40.

mp 6

    O Jacob, who do seek thy face   *mp*
      with their whole heart's desire.   2

mf 7 Ye gates, lift up your heads on high;
      ye doors that last for aye,
    Be lifted up, that so the King   *m* 3
      of glory enter may.

p 8 But who of glory is the King?   *mp*
f   THE MIGHTY LORD IS THIS;
    Ev'N THAT SAME LORD, THAT GREAT IN
    AND STRONG IN BATTLE IS.   [MIGHT

mf 9 Ye gates, lift up your heads; •ye doors,
      doors that do last for aye,
    Be lifted up, that so the King
      of glory enter may.

p 10 But who is he that is the King   *mp*
      of glory? who is this?
ff   THE LORD OF HOSTS, AND NONE BUT HE,
    THE KING OF GLORY IS.

PSALM XXV.

Ver. 1-7 *Selma* 166.   *Ludlow* 175.
Ver. 8-15 *Prague* 157.   *Dresden* 160.
Ver. 16-22 *Wirksworth* 174.   *St. Bride* 173.

∧   After thy mercy think on me,
    and for thy goodness great.

m 8 God good and upright is:
    the way he'll sinners show.

  9 The meek in judgment he will guide,   ∧ 15
    and make his path to know.

 10 The whole paths of the Lord   *mf*
    are truth and mercy sure,
    To those that do his cov'nant keep,   ∨ 16
    and testimonies pure.

p 11 *Now, for thine own name's sake,*   *p*
    O Lord, I thee entreat
    To pardon mine iniquity;   *pp* 17
    for it is very great.

m 12 What man is he that fears   ∧ 18
    the Lord, and doth him serve?
    Him shall he teach the way that he   *mp*19
    shall choose, and still observe.

 13 His soul shall dwell at ease·
    and his posterity
    Shall flourish still, and of the earth   *m* 20
    inheritors shall be.

:

,

:

∧ And let me never be asham'd   *mp* 6
     because I trust in thee.
21 Let uprightness and truth   ∧
     keep me, who thee attend.
∨ 22 Redemption, Lord, to Israel   *p* 7
     from all his troubles send.

Another of the same.   ∧

Ver. 1-7 *Morven* 99.   *Martyrdom* 64.
Ver. 8-15 *St. Andrew* 72.   *Newington* 63.   *m* 8
Ver. 16-22 *St. Neot* 150.   *Crowle* 153.

mp 1 TO thee I lift my soul, O Lord: :
   2   My God, I trust in thee:
∧   Let me not be asham'd; let not   9
     my foes triumph o'er me.
m 3 Yea, let thou none ashamed be
     that do on thee attend:
p   *Ashamed let them be, O Lord,*   10
     who without cause offend.

m 4 Thy ways, Lord, shew; teach me thy
   5   Lead me in truth, teach me: [paths:
     For of my safety thou art God;   *p* 11
     all day I wait on thee.

V *To pardon mine iniquity;*
   for it is very great.
m 12 What man fears God? him shall he teach
     the way that he shall choose.

13 His soul shall dwell at ease; his seed
   the earth, as heirs, shall use.

mp14 The secret of the Lord is with
     such as do fear his name·
     And he his holy covenant
     will manifest to them.

Λ 15 Towards the Lord my waiting eyes
     continually are set;
mf   For he it is that shall bring forth
      my feet out of the net.

V 16 O turn thee unto me, O God
     have mercy me upon;
     Because I solitary am,
     and in affliction.
pp 17 *Enlarg'd the griefs are of mine heart;*
      me from distress relieve.
Λ 18 See mine affliction and my pain,
     and all my sins forgive.

mp19

m 20

21
Λ
V 22

m 1   :

p 2

          :

∧ 3 For thy love is before mine eyes,
    thy truth's paths I have trode.

m 4 With persons vain I have not sat
    nor with dissemblers gone:

5 Th' assembly of ill men I hate;
    to sit with such I shun.

6 Mine hands in innocence, O Lord
    I'll wash and purify;
∧ So to thine holy altar go,
    and compass it will I:

f 7 THAT I, WITH VOICE OF THANKSGIVING
    MAY PUBLISH AND DECLARE,
    AND TELL OF ALL THY MIGHTY WORKS,
    THAT GREAT AND WONDROUS ARE.

mf 8 The habitation of thy house,
    Lord, I have loved well·
    Yea, in that place I do delight
    where doth thine honour dwell.

mp 9 With sinners gather not my soul,
    and such as blood would spill:

10 Whose hands mischievous plots, right
    corrupting bribes do fill.   [hand

mf 11 :

mp

mf 12 :

∧

PSALM XXVII.

Ver. 1-6 *Coleshill* 146.   *Durham* 95.
Ver. 7-14 *Ballerma* 114.   *Morven* 99.

f 1

m 2

f 3 AGAINST ME THOUGH AN HOST ENCAMP,
 MY HEART YET FEARLESS IS:
 THOUGH WAR AGAINST ME RISE, I WILL *mp* 7
 BE CONFIDENT IN THIS.

mp 4 One thing I of the Lord desir'd,
 and will seek to obtain,
 That all days of my life I may
 within God's house remain;

 That I the beauty of the Lord
 behold may and admire,
V And that I in his holy place *p* 9
 may rev'rently enquire.

Λ 5 For he in his pavilion shall
 me hide in evil days; Λ
 In secret of his tent me hide,
 and on a rock me raise.

m 6 And now, ev'n at this present time, *m* 10
 mine head shall lifted be
 Above all those that are my foes, 11
 and round encompass me: V
f THEREFORE UNTO HIS TABERNACLE
 I'LL SACRIFICES BRING

m 12 Give me not to mine en'mies' will;
 for witnesses that lie
 Against me risen are, and such   3
  as breathe out cruelty.

mp 13 I fainted had, unless that I
 believed had to see
 The Lord's own goodness in the land   4
  of them that living be.

mf 14 Wait on the Lord, and be thou strong
 and he shall strength afford
 Unto thine heart; yea, do thou wait,   *m* 5
 I say, upon the Lord.

PSALM XXVIII.

Ver. 1-5 St. Chad 152.   *Walsal 155.*   *mf* 6
Ver. 6-9 Gloucester 54.   *Tiverton 59.*

m 1 TO thee I'll cry, O Lord, my rock;
 hold not thy peace to me;
p   Lest like those that to pit descend   7
 I by thy silence be.
mp 2 The voice hear of my humble pray'rs,
 when unto thee I cry;

AND WITH MY SONG I WILL HIM PRAISE.

mf 8   Their strength is God alone:
    He also is the saving strength
      of his anointed one.

9 O thine own people do thou save,
    bless thine inheritance·
    Them also do thou feed, AND THEM
    FOR EVERMORE ADVANCE.

PSALM XXIX.

Old 29th 31.   *Salisbury* 55.

f 1 GIVE ye unto the Lord, ye sons
    that of the mighty be,
    All strength and glory to the Lord
    with cheerfulness give ye.
2 Unto the Lord the glory give
    that to his name is due;
mp *And in the beauty of holiness*
    unto JEHOVAH bow.

f 3 The Lord's voice on the waters is;
    the God of majesty

f 4

f 5

6

7
8

9

:

ff 10 The Lord sits on the floods; the
  sits King, and ever shall. [Lord
V 11 The Lord will give his people strength,
  and with peace bless them all.

∧ 5

p
f
m 6

PSALM XXX.

St. Ann 60. *St. Alphage* 118.

m 1 LORD, I will thee extol, for thou
  hast lifted me on high,
  And over me thou to rejoice
  mad'st not mine enemy.

7

p

  2 O thou who art the Lord my God,
V I in distress to thee,
∧ With loud cries lifted up my voice,
  and thou hast healed me.

p 8

mp 3 O Lord, my soul thou hast brought up,
  and rescu'd from the grave;
  That I to pit should not go down,
  alive thou didst me save.

9

mf 4 O ye that are his holy ones,
  sing praise unto the Lord;

∧

:

*mp*10 Hear, Lord, have mercy; help me, Lord:
  11   Thou turned hast my sadness
      To dancing; yea, my sackcloth loos'd,
      and girded me with gladness;

f 12 THAT SING THY PRAISE MY GLORY MAY,
     AND NEVER SILENT BE.
    O LORD MY GOD, FOR EVERMORE
    I WILL GIVE THANKS TO THEE.

PSALM XXXI.

Ver. 1-8 Durham 95.   York 46.
Ver. 9-13 Bangor 147.   Dundee 144.
Ver. 14-18 Old Carlisle 129.   St. Mary 145.
Ver. 19-24 Newington 63.   St. David 48.

mp 6

m 1 IN thee, O Lord, I put my trust,
    sham'd let me never be;
    According to thy righteousness
    ' do thou deliver me.

f

mp 2 Bow down thine ear to me, with speed
    send me deliverance:
m   To save me, my strong rock be thou,
    and my house of defence.

	And by thee have my feet been made in a large room to stand.	*mf* 14	
p	9 *O Lord, upon me mercy have,* *for trouble is on me:*		
	Mine eye, my belly, and my soul, *with grief consumed be.*	*mp*15	:
	10 *Because my life with grief is spent,* *my years with sighs and groans:*		
pp	*My strength doth fail; and for my sin* *consumed are my bones.*	16	:
*mp*11	I was a scorn to all my foes, and to my friends a fear;		
	And specially reproach'd of those that were my neighbours near·	17	:
	When they me saw they from me fled.	*p*	
	12 Ev'n so I am forgot,		
	As men are out of mind when dead: I'm like a broken pot.	18	
	13 For slanders I of many heard; fear compass'd me, while they		
	Against me did consult, and plot to take my life away.	*mf* 19	

And wrought'st for them that trust in
   the sons of men before!   [thee

mp 20 In secret of thy presence thou   *mp*
   shalt hide them from man's pride:
  From strife of tongues thou closely
   as in a tent, them hide.   [shalt,

f 21 ALL PRAISE AND THANKS BE TO THE
   FOR HE HATH MAGNIFY'D   [LORD;
  HIS WONDROUS LOVE TO ME WITHIN
  A CITY FORTIFY'D.

p 22 *For from thine eyes cut off I am,*   *p* 3
   I in my haste had said;
mp   My voice yet heard'st thou, when to thee
   with cries my moan I made.

m 23 O love the Lord, all ye his saints;   *pp*
   because the Lord doth guard
  The faithful, and he plenteously
   proud doers doth reward.

mf 24 Be of good courage, and he strength   *p*
   unto your heart shall send,
  All ye whose hope and confidence
   doth on the Lord depend.

      I will confess unto the Lord
        my trespasses, said I;
∧   And of my sin thou freely didst   *pp* 10
        forgive th' iniquity

m 6 For this shall ev'ry godly one   *m*
        his prayer make to thee;   ∧
      In such a time he shall thee seek   *f* 11
        as found thou mayest be.
      Surely, when floods of waters great
        do swell up to the brim,
∧   They shall not overwhelm his soul,
        nor once come near to him.

m 7 Thou art my hiding-place, thou shalt
        from trouble keep me free:
∧   Thou with songs of deliverance   *mf* 1
        about shalt compass me.

mp 8 I will instruct thee, and thee teach
        the way that thou shalt go;
      And, with mine eye upon thee set,   *f* 2
        I will direction show.

     9 Then be not like the horse or mule
        which do not understand;

∧	3	A new song to him sing, and play with loud noise skilfully;	*f*	
∨	4	For right is God's word, all his works are done in verity.	*m* 10	

m	5	To judgment and to righteousness
		    a love he beareth still;
		The loving-kindness of the Lord
		    the earth throughout doth fill.
			mf 11	

f				

m	6	The heavens by the word of God
		    did their beginning take;
		And by the breathing of his mouth
		    he all their hosts did make.
			∧
			f 12	

	7	The waters of the seas he brings
		    together as an heap;
		And in storehouses, as it were
		    he layeth up the deep.
			m 13	:

p	8	*Let earth, and all that live therein*
		    with rev'rence fear the Lord:
		Let all the world's inhabitants
		    dread him with one accord.
			14
			
			15	

m	9	For he did speak the word, and done it was without delay;	`16	

PSALMS XXXIII.

17 An horse for preservation   2
   is a deceitful thing;   V
  And by the greatness of his strength   ƒ 3
   can no deliv'rance bring.   Λ

18 Behold, on those that do him fear   m 4
   the Lord doth set his eye;   Λ
Λ Ev'n those who on his mercy do   m 5
   with confidence rely.

m 19 From death to free their soul in dearth Λ 6
   life unto them to yield.

ƒ 20 Our soul doth wait upon the Lord;   mf 7
   he is our help and shield.

Λ 21 Sith in his holy name we trust,
   OUR HEART SHALL JOYFUL BE.

V 22 Lord, let thy mercy be on us   mp 8
   as we do hope in thee.

               Λ 9

PSALM XXXIV.

Ver. 1-10 Chingford 91   Bedford 61.
Ver. 11-22 St. Matthew 39. Old 137th 35.   mp 10

mf 1 GOD will I bless all times; his praise ƒ
Λ   my mouth shall still express.

*mp*11 O children, hither do ye come,
and unto me give ear;

m   I shall you teach to understand
how ye the Lord should fear.

*mp*12 What man is he that life desires
to see good would live long?

m 13 Thy lips refrain from speaking guile,
and from ill words thy tongue.

14 Depart from ill, do good, seek peace,
pursue it earnestly.

15 God's eyes are on the just; his ears
are open to their cry.

*mp*16 The face of God is set against
those that do wickedly,
That he may quite out from the earth
cut off their memory.

17 The righteous cry unto the Lord,
he unto them gives ear;
And they out of their troubles all
by him deliver'd are.

*mp*18 The Lord is ever nigh to them
that be of broken sp'rit;

p 19

f

m 20

p 21

22
ff

m 1 PLE

2

PSALM XXXV

mf 3 Draw also out the spear, and do
against them stop the way
That me pursue: unto my soul,
I'm thy salvation, say.

4 Let them confounded be and sham'd
that for my soul have sought:
Who plot my hurt turn'd back be they,
and to confusion brought.

5 Let them be like unto the chaff
that flies before the wind;
And let the angel of the Lord
pursue them hard behind.

6 With darkness cover thou their way,
and let it slipp'ry prove;
And let the angel of the Lord
pursue them from above.

m 7 For without cause have they for me
their net hid in a pit,
They also have without a cause
for my soul digged it.

8 Let ruin seize him unawares·
his net he hid withal

f 9

10

m

11

12

p 13

14

:

*mp*15 But in my trouble **they** rejoic'd,
  gath'ring themselves **together**;
 Yea, abjects vile together did
  themselves against **me** gather: *p* 21   *'gainst me*
 I knew it not; they did **me** tear,
  and quiet would **not** be.   *m* 22
16 With mocking hypocrites, **at feasts**
  they gnash'd their teeth at **me**.   ⋀ 23

17 How long, Lord, look'st thou on? from
⋀ destructions they intend   [those
 Rescue my soul, from lions young   *mf* 24
  my darling do defend.
f 18 I will give thanks to thee, O Lord,
  within th' assembly great;
 And where much people gather'd are   25
  thy praises forth will set.

m 19 Let not my wrongful enemies
  proudly rejoice o'er me;
 Nor who me hate without a cause,   26
  let them wink with the eye.
20 For peace they do not speak at all;

∧
∨ 27 Let them that love my righteous cause
   BE GLAD, SHOUT, AND NOT CEASE
   TO SAY, THE LORD BE MAGNIFY'D,
    who loves his servant's peace.

f 28 THY RIGHTEOUSNESS SHALL ALSO BE
   DECLARED BY MY TONGUE;
   THE PRAISES THAT BELONG TO THEE
   SPEAK SHALL IT ALL DAY LONG.

PSALM XXXVI.

Ver. 1-4 *St. Paul* 50.   *Ballerma* 114.
Ver. 5-12 *New London* 53.   *St. Stephen* 62.

p 1 THE wicked man's transgression
   within my heart thus says,
Undoubtedly the fear of God
   is not before his eyes.
2 Because himself he flattereth
   in his own blinded eye,
Until the hatefulness be found
   of his iniquity.
3 Words from his mouth proceeding are,
   fraud and iniquity:

4

mf 5

∧ 6

mp 7

mf

8

∧

m 9

∧

:

*mp*10 Thy loving-kindness unto them
  continue that thee know;
  And still on men upright in heart
   thy righteousness bestow.

11 Let not the foot of cruel pride
  come, and against me stand:
  And let me not removed be,
  Lord, by the wicked's hand.

12 There fallen are they, and ruined
  that work iniquities:
  Cast down they are, and never shall
  be able to arise.

PSALM XXXVII
Abbey 56. St. Simon 43.

mp 1 FOR evil-doers, fret thou not
  thyself unquietly;
  Nor do thou envy bear to those
  that work iniquity.

p 2 For, even like unto the grass,
  soon be cut down shall they;
  And, like the green and tender herb,
  they wither shall away.

m 3 Set thou thy trust upon the Lord
  and be thou doing good;
  And so thou in the land shalt dwell
  and verily have food.

mf 4 Delight thyself in God; he'll give
  thine heart's desire to thee.

5 Thy way to God commit, him trust
  it bring to pass shall he.

6 And, like unto the light, he shall
  thy righteousness display;
  AND HE THY JUDGMENT SHALL BRING
  LIKE NOON-TIDE OF THE DAY. [FORTH

mp 7 Rest in the Lord, and patiently
  wait for him: do not fret
  For him who, prosp'ring in his way,
  success in sin doth get.

m 8 Do thou from anger cease, and wrath
  see thou forsake also:
  Fret not thyself in any wise,
  that evil thou should'st do.

p 9 For those that evil-doers are
  shall be cut off and fall:

f
∧ BUT THOSE THAT WAIT UPON THE LORD
   THE EARTH INHERIT SHALL.   *m* 16

p 10 For yet a little while, and then
   the wicked shall not be;
   His place thou shalt consider well,   ∧ 17
   but it thou shalt not see.

m 11 But by inheritance the earth   *mf* 18
   the meek ones shall possess:
∧   They also shall delight themselves   19
   in an abundant peace.

p 12 The wicked plots against the just,
   and at him whets his teeth:

mf 13 The Lord shall laugh at him, because   *pp* 20
   his day he coming seeth.   ∧
                    V

p 14 The wicked have drawn out the sword,
   and bent their bow, to slay
   The poor and needy, and to kill   *p* 21
   men of an upright way.

15 But their own sword, which they have   *m*
   shall enter their own heart: [drawn,
∧   Their bows which they have bent shall   *mf* 22
   and into pieces part.   [break,

p	And they that cursed are of him shall be destroyed all.	m 29	:
m 23	A good man's footsteps by the Lord are ordered aright;	30	
	And in the way wherein he walks he greatly doth delight.	31	
24	Although he fall, yet shall he not be cast down utterly;	mp32	
∧	Because the Lord with his own hand upholds him mightily.	m 33	:
m 25	I have been young, and now am old, yet have I never seen		
	The just man left, nor that his seed for bread have beggars been.	∧ 34	
26	He's ever merciful, and lends: his seed is bless'd therefore.	∨	
27	Depart from evil, and do good, and dwell for evermore.	m 35	,
28	For God loves judgment, and his saints leaves not in any case:	p 36	:
	They are kept ever: *but cut off*	mf 37	
pp	*shall be the sinner's race.*		

Ⅴ Because that surely of this man
    the latter end is peace.

p 2

3

*mp*38 But those men that transgressors are
    shall be destroy'd together·
Ⅴ *The latter end of wicked men*
    shall be cut off for ever.

mf 39 But the salvation of the just
    is from the Lord above;
    He in the time of their distress
    their stay and strength doth prove.·

4

f 40 THE LORD SHALL HELP, AND THEM DELI-
    HE SHALL THEM FREE AND SAVE [VER:
    FROM WICKED MEN; BECAUSE IM HIM

5

    THEIR CONFIDENCE THEY HAVE.

6

PSALM XXXVIII.

7

Bangor 147.   *Dundee* 144.

pp 1 IN thy great indignation,
    O Lord, rebuke me not;
Λ *Nor on me lay thy chast'ning hand,*
Ⅴ   *in thy displeasure hot.*

8

:

	That, through disquiet of my heart,	14	
	I have been made to roar.		
m 9	O Lord, all that I do desire	*mf* 15	
	is still before thine eye;		
V	And of my heart the secret groans	*m* 16	
	not hidden are from thee.		
p 10	My heart doth pant incessantly,		
	my strength doth quite decay;		
	As for mine eyes, their wonted light	*p* 17	
	is from me gone away.		
11	My lovers and my friends do stand	18	
	at distance from my sore;		
	And those do stand aloof that were	19	
	kinsmen and kind before.		
12	Yea, they that seek my life lay snares:		
	who seek to do me wrong		
	Speak things mischievous, and deceits	20	
	imagine all day long.		
13	But, as one deaf, that heareth not,	*m*	
	I suffer'd all to pass;		
	I as a dumb man did become,	21	
	whose mouth not open'd was:		

⋀ 22 O Lord, thou my salvation art,
      haste to give help to me.   5

PSALM XXXIX.

St. Mary 145.   *St. Neot* 150.   *p* 6

m 1 I SAID, I will look to my ways,
      lest with my tongue I sin:
    In sight of wicked men my mouth
      with bridle I'll keep in.   *mp* 7

p 2 With silence I as dumb became
      I did myself restrain   ⋀ 8
    From speaking good; but then the more
      increased was my pain.   *p* 9

  3 My heart within me waxed hot·   10
⋀   and, while I musing was,
    The fire did burn; and from my tongue 11
⋁   these words I did let pass:

pp 4 *Mine end, and measure of my days,*   *pp*
      O Lord, unto me show
    What is the same; that I thereby   *m* 12
      my frailty well may know.

p   I sojourn as my fathers all,
     and stranger am with thee.

⋀ 13 O spare thou me, that I my strength
     recover may again,
⋁   Before from hence I do depart
    and here no more remain.

4

5

PSALM XL.

Ver. 1-5 *Ballerma* 114.   *Prestwich* 113.
Ver. 6-10 *St. Thomas* 75.   *Stafford* 94.
Ver. 11-17 *Silesia* 149.   *St. Mary* 145.

p 1 *I WAITED for the Lord my God,*
     and patiently did bear;
⋀   At length to me he did incline
     my voice and cry to hear.
mp 2 He took me from a fearful pit
     and from the miry clay,
⋀   And on a rock he set my feet,
     establishing my way.
mf 3 He put a new song in my mouth,
     our God to magnify:

far

m 6

mp 7

:

:

PSALM XL.

   8 To do thy will I take delight
      O thou my God that art;   V
     Yea, that most holy law of thine
      I have within my heart.

m 9 Within the congregation great   *mp*13
     I righteousness did preach:
     Lo, thou dost know, O Lord, that I   *mf* 14
      refrained not my speech.

 10 I never did within my heart
     conceal thy righteousness;
     I thy salvation have declar'd,   15
      and shown thy faithfulness:
     Thy kindness, which most loving is,
      concealed have not I,
     Nor from the congregation great   *f* 16
      have hid thy verity.

 11 Thy tender mercies, Lord, from me
     O do thou not restrain:
     Thy loving-kindness, and thy truth   *p* 17
      let them me still maintain.
p 12 *For ills past reck'ning compass me,*
     and mine iniquities

PSALM XLI.

Ver. 1-3 *St. David* 48.   *Lancaster* 68.
Ver. 4-13 *Dundee* 144.   *Martyrdom* 64.

6

m 1 BLESSED is he that wisely doth
   the poor man's case consider·
For when the time of trouble is,
   the Lord will him deliver.

7

2 God will him keep, yea, save alive;
   on earth he bless'd shall live·

8

And to his enemies' desire
   thou wilt him not up give.

p 9

3 God will give strength when he on bed
   of languishing doth mourn;
And in his sickness sore, O Lord
   thou all his bed wilt turn.

mf 10

4 I said, O Lord, do thou extend
   thy mercy unto me;
> O do thou heal my soul; for why?
p   *I have offended thee.*

11

mp 5 Those that to me are enemies,
   of me do evil say;

12 But as for me, thou me uphold'st
   in mine integrity;
∧ And me before thy countenance   4
   thou sett'st continually.
f 13 THE LORD, THE GOD OF ISRAEL
   BE BLESS'D FOR EVER THEN,
   FROM AGE TO AGE ETERNALLY.
   AMEN, YEA, AND AMEN.

PSALM XLII.

Ver. 1-7 *Harrington* 120.   *York Minster* 134.
Ver. 8-11 *Philippi* 116.   *Old Carlisle* 129.

mp 1 LIKE as the hart for water-brooks
∧   in thirst doth pant and bray;
   So pants my longing soul, O God,
   that come to thee I may.
m 2 My soul for God, the living God,
   doth thirst: when shall I near
   Unto thy countenance approach,
   and in God's sight appear?

p 3 My tears have unto me been meat
   both in the night and day,

:

∧

p 5

f .

p 6

∧
  7

V

mf 8 His loving-kindness yet the Lord
　　　command will in the day,
　　His song's with me by night; to God   *m* 1
　　　by whom I live, I'll pray:
　　9 And I will say to God my rock,
v　　　Why me forgett'st thou so?
p　　*Why, for my foes' oppression,*   2
　　　thus mourning do I go?

　　10 'Tis as a sword within my bones,
　　　when my foes me upbraid
　　Ev'n when by them, Where is thy God?   *m* 3
　　　'tis daily to me said.
　　11 O why art thou cast down, my soul?
　　　why, thus with grief opprest,
　　Art thou disquieted in me?   *f* 4
　　　in God still hope and rest:

mf　　For yet I know I shall him praise,
　　　who graciously to me
　　The health is of my countenance,   *mp* 5
　　　yea, mine own God is he.

disquieted in me?

mf
Λ Still trust in God; for him to praise
GOOD CAUSE I YET SHALL HAVE:
HE OF MY COUNT'NANCE IS THE HEALTH,
MY GOD THAT DOTH ME SAVE.

f 5

6

PSALM XLIV.

Ver. 1-8 Old 44th 32. Martyrs 148.
Ver. 9-26 Dundee 144. Crowle 153.

7

mf 1 O GOD, we with our ears have heard,
our fathers have us told,
What works thou in their days hadst
ev'n in the days of old.   [done,
2 Thy hand did drive the heathen out,
and plant them in their place;
p   Thou didst afflict the nations,
mf   but them thou didst increase.

8

mp 9

10

3 For neither got their sword the land,
nor did their arm them save;
f   But thy right hand, arm, countenance;
for thou them favour gave.
m 4 Thou art my King: for Jacob, Lord,
deliv'rances command.

p 11

*mp*12

13 Thou mak'st us a reproach to be
 unto our neighbours near;
 Derision and a scorn to them
 that round about us are.

14 A by-word also thou dost us
 among the heathen make;
 The people, in contempt and spite,
 at us their heads do shake.

15 Before me my confusion
 continually abides;
 And of my bashful countenance
 the shame me ever hides:

16 For voice of him that doth reproach,
 and speaketh blasphemy;
 By reason of th' avenging foe,
 and cruel enemy.

m ⟨ 17 All this is come on us, yet we
 have not forgotten thee;
 Nor falsely in thy covenant
 behav'd ourselves have we.

18 Back from thy way our heart not turn'd;
 our steps no straying made;

⋁	19
m	20
	21
mp	22
mf	23
	24
⋁	25
p	
mf.	26

:

PSALM XLV.

PSALM XLV.

m 1 MY heart brings forth a goodly thing;
    my words that I indite
Concern the King: my tongue's a pen   *mf* 7
    of one that swift doth write.
  2 Thou fairer art than sons of men: oil
    into thy lips is store
Of grace infus'd; God therefore thee   8
    hath bless'd for evermore.

f 3 O THOU THAT ART THE MIGHTY ONE,
    THY SWORD GIRD ON THY THIGH;
Ev'N WITH THY GLORY EXCELLENT,   9   :
    AND WITH THY MAJESTY.
mf 4 For meekness, truth, and righteousness,
    in state ride prosp'rously;
And thy right hand shall thee instruct   *mp*10
    in things that fearful be.

m 5 Thine arrows sharply pierce the heart
    of th' en'mies of the King;
And under thy subjection   *mf* 11   :
    the people down do bring.
f 6 FOR EVER AND FOR EVER IS,
    O GOD, THY THRONE OF MIGHT;

m 12 The daughter there of Tyre shall be
  with gifts and off'rings great:
  Those of the people that are rich
  thy favour shall entreat.

mf 13 Behold, the daughter of the King
  all glorious is within;
  And with embroideries of gold
  her garments wrought have been.

f 14 SHE SHALL BE BROUGHT UNTO THE KING
  IN ROBES WITH NEEDLE WROUGHT;
  HER FELLOW-VIRGINS FOLLOWING
  SHALL UNTO THEE BE BROUGHT.

ff 15 THEY SHALL BE BROUGHT WITH GLADNESS
  AND MIRTH ON EV'RY SIDE, [GREAT,
  INTO THE PALACE OF THE KING,
  AND THERE THEY SHALL ABIDE.

mp 16 Instead of those thy fathers dear
  thy children thou may'st take
 Λ And in all places of the earth
  them noble princes make.

mf 17 Thy name remember'd I will make
 Λ through ages all to be:

THE PEOPLE THEREFORE EVERMORE
SHALL PRAISES GIVE TO THEE.

m 1

:   made,
:

2   :

f 3   :

mf 4 For meekness, truth, and right,
      ride prosp'rously in state;
    And thy right hand shall teach to thee
      things terrible and great.
m 5 Thy shafts shall pierce their hearts
      that foes are to the King;
    Whereby into subjection
      the people thou shalt bring.
f 6 THY ROYAL SEAT, O LORD,
      FOR EVER SHALL REMAIN:
    THE SCEPTRE OF THY KINGDOM DOTH
      ALL RIGHTEOUSNESS MAINTAIN.
mf 7 Thou lov'st right, and bat'st ill;
      for God, thy God, most high,
    Above thy fellows hath with th' oil
      of joy anointed thee.
   8 Of myrrh and spices sweet
      a smell thy garments had,
    Out of the iv'ry palaces,
      whereby they made thee glad.
   9 And in thy glorious train
      kings' daughters waiting stand;

mp 10

mf 11

mp

m 12

mf 13

f 14

ff 15 THEY SHALL BE BROUGHT WITH JOY,
 AND MIRTH ON EV'RY SIDE,
 INTO THE PALACE OF THE KING,   *mf* 4
 AND THERE THEY SHALL ABIDE.

*mp*16 And in thy fathers' stead,
 thy children thou may'st take,
 And in all places of the earth   *f* 5
 them noble princes make.
mf 17 I will shew forth thy name
 to generations all·
 THEREFORE THE PEOPLE EVERMORE   *mf* 6
 TO THEE GIVE PRAISES SHALL.

           p
           mf 7

PSALM XLVI.

Stroudwater 74. Montrose 49.

f 1 GOD is our refuge and our strength,
 in straits a present aid;
ff 2 THEREFORE, ALTHOUGH THE EARTH RE-
 WE WILL NOT BE AFRAID: [MOVE,
 THOUGH HILLS AMIDST THE SEAS BE CAST;
 3 THOUGH WATERS ROARING MAKE,

PSALMS XLVI.

mf 9 Unto the ends of all the earth
    wars into peace he turns·
    The bow he breaks, the spear he cuts,
      in fire the chariot burns.

p 10 *Be still, and know that I am God;*
Λ   *among the heathen I*
    Will be exalted; I on earth
f   will be exalted high.
 11 OUR GOD, WHO IS THE LORD OF HOSTS
Λ   IS STILL UPON OUR SIDE;
    THE GOD OF JACOB OUR REFUGE
    FOR EVER WILL ABIDE.

PSALM XLVII.

St. Magnus 45.   *Montrose 49.*   *Old 44th 32.*

f 1 ALL people, clap your hands; to God
    with voice of triumph shout
mp 2 *For dreadful is the Lord most high*
mf   *great King the earth throughout.*
 3 The heathen people under us
Λ   be surely shall subdue:

mf 4

ff 5

6

mf 7

8

9

Λ   :

PSALM XLVIII.

St. Magnus 45.   Montrose 49.

mf 1 GREAT is the Lord, and greatly he
    is to be praised still,
Within the city of our God
    upon his holy hill.

2 Mount Sion stands most beautiful
    the joy of all the land;
The city of the mighty King
    on her north side doth stand.

3 The Lord within her palaces
    is for a refuge known.
mp 4 *For, lo, the kings that gather'd were*
    together, by have gone.
5 *But when they did behold the same,*
    they, wond'ring, would not stay;
But, being troubled at the sight,
    they thence did haste away.

p 6 *Great terror there took hold on them*
    they were possess'd with fear;
Their grief came like a woman's pain,
    when she a child doth bear.

m 7
   8

   9
m 10

mf 11

   12

   13

   14

Our God for evermore; he will
V   ev'n unto death us guide.

PSALM XLIX.
Evan 125.   St. Mary 145.

m 1 HEAR this, all people, and give ear,
     all in the world that dwell;
   2 Both low and high, both rich and poor.
   3   My mouth shall wisdom tell:
     My heart shall knowledge meditate.
   4   I will incline mine ear
     To parables, and on the harp
     my sayings dark declare.
   5 Amidst those days that evil be,
     why should I, fearing, doubt?
     When of my heels th' iniquity
     shall compass me about.
   6 Whoe'er they be that in their wealth
     their confidence do pitch,
     And boast themselves, because they are
     become exceeding rich:

mp 7 Yet none of these his brother can
     redeem by any way;
     Nor can he unto God for him
     sufficient ransom pay,
p 8 (*Their soul's redemption precious is,*
Λ   and it can never be,)
   9 That still he should for ever live,
     and not corruption see.
m 10 For why? he seeth that wise men die,
     and brutish fools also
     Do perish; and their wealth, when dead
     to others they let go.
   11 Their inward thought is, that their house
     and dwelling-places shall
     Stand through all ages; they their lands
     by their own names do call.
   12 But yet in honour shall not man
     abide continually;
V   But passing hence, may be compar'd
     unto the beasts that die.
m 13 Thus brutish folly plainly is
     their wisdom and their way;

Yet their posterity approve
    what they do fondly say.
p 14 *Like sheep they in the grave are laid,*
    and death shall them devour;
∧ And in the morning upright men
    shall over them have pow'r:
p *Their beauty from their dwelling shall*
    consume within the grave.
∧ 15 But from hell's hand God will me free
∧   for he shall me receive.
m 16 Be thou not then afraid when one
    enriched thou dost see,
Nor when the glory of his house
    advanced is on high:
17 For he shall carry nothing hence
    when death his days doth end·
Nor shall his glory after him
    into the grave descend.
18 Although he his own soul did bless
    whilst he on earth did live;
(And when thou to thyself dost well,
    men will thee praises give;)

mp 19

20   is

f 1   sun,

2

3   :

∧

mf 4

	And to the earth likewise, that he may judge his people all.	*m* 11	
	5 Together let my saints unto me gather'd be,		
	Those that by sacrifice have made a covenant with me.	12	
f	6 And then the heavens shall his righteousness declare:	⋀	
	Because the Lord himself is he by whom men judged are.	*m* 13	
m	7 My people Isr'el hear, speak will I from on high,	14	
	Against thee I will testify; God, ev'n thy God, am I.	*mp*15	
	8 I for thy sacrifice no blame will on thee lay,	⋀	
	Nor for burnt-off'rings, which to me thou offer'dst ev'ry day.	*mf* 16	
	9 I'll take no calf nor goats from house or fold of thine:		
⋀	10 For beasts of forests, cattle all on thousand hills, are mine.	*m* 17	

And sith my words behind thy back | *mf* 23
thou cast'st, and dost reject.
mp 18 When thou a thief didst see,
with him thou didst consent;
p　*And with the vile adulterers*
partaker on thou went.

m 19 Thou giv'st thy mouth to ill,
thy tongue deceit doth frame;
20 Thou sitt'st, and 'gainst thy brother | *mf* 1
thy mother's son dost shame. [speak'st,
mp 21 Because I silence kept,
while thou these things hast wrought;
That I was altogether like
thyself, hath been thy thought:

mf　Yet I will thee reprove,
and set before thine eyes,
In order ranked, thy misdeeds, | 3
and thine iniquities.
p 22 *Now, ye that God forget,*
this carefully consider;
Lest I in pieces tear you all, | *mf* 4
and none can you deliver.

Another of the same.

Shall call, that he his judgments may
 before his people show.

5 Let all my saints together be
 unto me gathered;
 Those that by sacrifice with me
 a covenant have made.

f 6 And then the heavens shall declare
 his righteousness abroad:
 Because the Lord himself doth come;
 none else is judge but God.

m 7 Hear, O my people, and I'll speak;
 O Israel by name,
 Against thee I will testify;
 God, ev'n thy God, I am.

8 I for thy sacrifices few
 reprove thee never will
 Nor for burnt-off'rings to have been
 before me offer'd still.

9 I'll take no bullock nor he-goats
 from house nor folds of thine:

⋀ 10 For beasts of forests, cattle all
 on thousand hills, are mine.

m 11

12

⋀

m 13

mf 14   :

           :

mp 15

⋀

mp 16

Of my commands? how dar'st thou in
    thy mouth my cov'nant take?   *p* 22

m 17 Sith it is so that thou dost hate
    all good instruction;
And sith thou cast'st behind thy back,   *mf* 23
    and slight'st my words each one.

  18 When thou a thief didst see, then straight
    thou join'dst with him in sin,
p   *And with the vile adulterers*
    thou hast partaker been.

m 19 Thy mouth to evil thou dost give,
    thy tongue deceit doth frame.

  20 Thou sitt'st, and 'gainst thy brother
    thy mother's son to shame. [speak'st,

*mp*21 These things thou wickedly hast done,
    and I have silent been:
Thou thought'st that I was like thyself,
    and did approve thy sin:
mf   But I will sharply thee reprove,   3
    and I will order right
Thy sins and thy transgressions   *p* 4
    in presence of thy sight.

PSALM LI.

Ver. 1-12 *Dundee* 144.   *Walsal* 155.
Ver 13-19 *St. Mary* 145   *Eversley* 108

PSALM LI.

That when thou speak'st thou may'st be
 and clear in judging still.   [just,

mp 5 Behold, I in iniquity
 was form'd the womb within·
 My mother also me conceiv'd
 in guiltiness and sin.

m 6 Behold, thou in the inward parts
 with truth delighted art;
Λ And wisdom thou shalt make me know
 within the hidden part.

m 7 Do thou with hyssop sprinkle me
 I shall be cleansed so;
Λ Yea, wash thou me, and then I shall
 be whiter than the snow.

mf 8 OF GLADNESS AND OF JOYFULNESS
 MAKE ME TO HEAR THE VOICE;
 THAT SO THESE VERY BONES WHICH THOU
 HAST BROKEN MAY REJOICE.

p 9 *All mine iniquities blot out,*
 thy face hide from my sin.

Λ 10 Create a clean heart, Lord, renew
 a right sp'rit me within.

p 11 *Cast me not from thy sight, nor take*
 thy Holy Sp'rit away.

Λ 12

mf 13

mp 14

mf

mp 15

mf

m 16

mp 17

a   .

A broken and a contrite heart,
    Lord, thou wilt not despise.

m 18 Shew kindness, and do good, O Lord,
    to Sion, thine own hill:
  The walls of thy Jerusalem   4
    build up of thy good will.

mf 19 THEN RIGHTEOUS OFF'RINGS SHALL THEE | mf
    PLEASE,
  AND OFF'RINGS BURNT, WHICH THEY
  WITH WHOLE BURNT OFF'RINGS, AND
    WITH CALVES, | mp
    SHALL ON THINE ALTAR LAY.

PSALM LII.

St. Nicholas 151.   Coleshill 146.

mf 1 WHY dost thou boast, O mighty man,
    of mischief and of ill?
  The goodness of Almighty God
    endureth ever still.

m 2 Thy tongue mischievous calumnies
    deviseth subtilely,

mf 9 And I for ever will thee praise,
  because thou hast done this:
m   I on thy name will wait; for good
  before thy saints it is.

PSALM LIII.

Stafford 94.   *St. Paul 50.*

m 1 THAT there is not a God, the fool
  doth in his heart conclude:
  They are corrupt, their works are vile,
  not one of them doth good.
  2 The Lord upon the sons of men
  from heav'n did cast his eyes,
  To see if any one there was
  that sought God, and was wise.
mp 3 They altogether filthy are,
  they all are backward gone;
  And there is none that doeth good
  no, not so much as one.
m 4 These workers of iniquity,
  do they not know at all,

mp 5

∧
∨
f 6
∧

PSALM LIV.

St. James 98.   *St. Chad 136.*

mp 1
∧ 2

3 For they that strangers are to me
　　do up against me rise;
V Oppressors seek my soul, and God
　　set not before their eyes.

mf 4 The Lord my God my helper is,
　　lo, therefore I am bold ·
　　He taketh part with ev'ry one
　　that doth my soul uphold.
m 5 Unto mine enemies he shall
　　mischief and ill repay:
Λ O for thy truth's sake cut them off,
　　and sweep them clean away.

mf 6 I will a sacrifice to thee
　　give with free willingness;
　　Thy name, O Lord, because 'tis good,
　　with praise I will confess.
7 For he hath me delivered
　　from all adversities;
　　And his desire mine eye hath seen
　　upon mine enemies.

m 1

Λ 2

V

mp 3

p 4
pp
　　5

mp 6

　　7

Λ 8 From windy storm and tempest I
     would haste to 'scape away.

f 9 O LORD, ON THEM DESTRUCTION BRING,
     AND DO THEIR TONGUES DIVIDE;

m   For in the city violence
     and strife I have espy'd.

  10 They day and night upon the walls
     do go about it round:
    There mischief is, and sorrow there
     in midst of it is found.

  11 Abundant wickedness there is
     within her inward part;
    And from her streets deceitfulness
     and guile do not depart.

*mp*12 He was no foe that me reproach'd,
     then that endure I could;
    Nor hater that did 'gainst me boast,
     from him me hide I would.

m 13 But thou, man, who mine equal, guide,
     and mine acquaintance wast:

  14 We join'd sweet counsels, to God's house
     in company we past.

mf 15

f 16
m 17

Λ

m 18

19

20 '

mp 21
Λ

mp   His speeches were more soft than oil,
∧   and yet drawn swords they are.

m 22 Cast thou thy burden on the Lord,
      and he shall thee sustain;
∧   Yea, he shall cause the righteous man
      unmoved to remain.

  23 But thou, O Lord my God, those men
      in justice shalt o'erthrow,
∨ And in destruction's dungeon dark
      at last shalt lay them low:

mp   The bloody and deceitful men
      shall not live half their days:
mf   But upon thee with confidence
      I will depend always.

PSALM LVI.

Coleshill 146.   *St. Nicholas 151.*

p 1 SHEW mercy, Lord, to me, for man
       would swallow me outright;
    He me oppresseth, while he doth
      against me daily fight.

2

∧ 3
∧ 4

m 5

p 6

∧ 7
mf

p 8

m 9
∧

:

DO,

10 In God his word I'll praise; his word
   in God shall praised be.
11 In God I trust; I will not fear
   what man can do to me.
mp 12 Thy vows upon me are, O God:
      I'll render praise to thee.

mp 13 Wilt thou not, who from death me sav'd,
      my feet from falls keep free,
   To walk before God in the light
      of those that living be?

PSALM LVII.

Ver. 1-6 *Martyrdom* 64.   *Ballerma* 114.
Ver. 7-11 *St. George* 52.   *York* 46.

p 1 *B*E *merciful to me, O God;*
         thy mercy unto me
      Do thou extend; because my soul
         doth put her trust in thee:
mp   Yea, in the shadow of thy wings
         my refuge I will place,
      Until these sad calamities
         do wholly overpass.

f

p

mf

8 My glory wake; wake psalt'ry, harp;
   myself I'll early raise.

9 I'll praise thee 'mong the people, Lord;
   'mong nations sing will I:
10 For great to heav'n thy mercy is,
   thy truth is to the sky.
11 O Lord, exalted be thy name
   above the heav'ns to stand:
   Do thou thy glory far advance
   above both sea and land.

PSALM LVIII.

Abbey 56.   *St. Simon 43.*

mp 1 DO ye, O congregation,
    indeed speak righteousness?
   O ye that are the sons of men,
    judge ye with uprightness?
mf 2 Yea, ev'n within your very hearts
   ye wickedness have done;
   And ye the vi'lence of your hands
   do weigh the earth upon.

m 3 The wicked men estranged are,
    ev'n from the very womb;
   They, speaking lies, do stray as soon
    as to the world they come.
4 Unto a serpent's poison like
   their poison doth appear;
   Yea, they are like the adder deaf,
   that closely stops her ear;

5 That so she may not hear the voice
   of one that charm her would,
   No, not though he most cunning were,
   and charm most wisely could.
mf 6 Their teeth, O God, within their mouth
   break thou in pieces small;
   The great teeth break thou out, O Lord,
   of these young lions all.

m 7 Let them like waters melt away,
   which downward still do flow:
   In pieces cut his arrows all,
   when he shall bend his bow.
8 Like to a snail that melts away,
   let each of them be gone;

Like woman's birth untimely, that
  they never see the sun.

9 He shall them take away before
  your pots the thorns can find
  Both living, and in fury great,
  as with a stormy wind.

mf 10 The righteous, when he vengeance sees,
  he shall be joyful then;
  The righteous one shall wash his feet
  in blood of wicked men.

11 So men shall say, The righteous man
  reward shall never miss:

f AND VERILY UPON THE EARTH
  A GOD TO JUDGE THERE IS.

PSALM LIX.

Bangor 147.   *Crowle 153.*

mp 1 MY God, deliver me from those
  that are mine enemies;
  And do thou me defend from those
  that up against me rise.

2

3   :

4   :

mf

5

mp 6

7   :

    For they do say thus, Who is he
      that now doth hear our words?

mf 8 But thou, O Lord, shalt laugh at them,
     and all the heathen mock.

   9 While he's in pow'r I'll wait on thee;
     for God is my high rock.

m 10 He of my mercy that is God
      betimes shall me prevent;
    Upon mine en'mies God shall let
     me see mine heart's content.

  11 Them slay not, lest my folk forget;
     but scatter them abroad
    By thy strong pow'r; and bring them
     O thou our shield and God. [down,

m 12 For their mouth's sin, and for the words
      that from their lips do fly,
    Let them be taken in their pride;
     because they curse and lie.

  13 In wrath consume them, them consume,
     that so they may not be:
    And that in Jacob God doth rule
     to th' earth's ends let them see.

m 14

mp 15

f 16

17

p 1

< *Thou justly hast displeased been ;*
 return to us, O God.   7

p 2 *The earth to tremble thou hast made :*
  therein didst breaches make :
◊ Do thou thereof the breaches heal,
  because the land doth shake.

3 Unto thy people thou hard things
  hast shew'd, and on them sent;
  And thou hast caused us to drink   *m* 9
  wine of astonishment.

m 4 And yet a banner thou hast giv'n
  to them who thee do fear;
  That it by them, because of truth,
  displayed may appear.

mp 5 That thy beloved people may
  deliver'd be from thrall,
◊ Save with the pow'r of thy right hand,   11
  and hear me when I call.

mf 6 God in his holiness hath spoke ;   *f* 12
  herein I will take pleasure :
  Shechem I will divide, and forth
  will Succoth's valley measure.

PSALM LXI.

Farrant 58.   St. Nicholas 151.

mp 1 O GOD, give ear unto my cry;
    unto my pray'r attend.

2 From th' utmost corner of the land
    my cry to thee I'll send.

p   *What time my heart is overwhelm'd,*
    and in perplexity,

  Do thou me lead unto the Rock
    that higher is than I.

m 3 For thou hast for my refuge been
    a shelter by thy pow'r;

  And for defence against my foes
    thou hast been a strong tow'r.

mf 4 Within thy tabernacle I
    for ever will abide;

  And under covert of thy wings
    with confidence me hide.

mp 5 For thou the vows that I did make,
    O Lord my God, didst hear:

  Thou hast giv'n me the heritage
    of those thy name that fear.

mp 3 How long will ye against a man
plot mischief? ye shall all
∧ Be slain; ye as a tott'ring fence
shall be, and bowing wall.

m 4 They only plot to cast him down
from his excellency:
They joy in lies; with mouth they
but they curse inwardly.   [bless,

mp 5 My soul, wait thou with patience
upon thy God alone;
∧ On him dependeth all my hope
and expectation.

mf 6 He only my salvation is,
. and my strong rock is he;
He only is my sure defence:
∧ I shall not moved be.

mf 7 In God my glory placed is,
and my salvation sure;
In God the rock is of my strength,
my refuge most secure.

m 8 Ye people, place your confidence
in him continually·

mp Before him pour ye out your heart:
f GOD IS OUR REFUGE HIGH.

p 9 *Surely mean men are vanity,*
and great men are a lie;
In balance laid, they wholly are
more light than vanity.

*mp*10 Trust ye not in oppression,
in robb'ry be not vain;
On wealth set not your hearts, when as
increased is your gain.

m 11 God hath it spoken once to me,
yea, this I heard again,
That power to Almighty God
alone doth appertain.

*mf*12 Yea, mercy also unto thee
belongs, O Lord, alone:
For thou according to his work
rewardest ev'ry one.

PSALM LXIII.
Denfield 124.   Caithness 126.

p 1 *L*ORD, *thee my God, I'll early seek:*
∧ *my soul doth thirst for thee;*

V	My flesh longs in a dry parch'd land,	*mp*	9
	wherein no waters be ·		
mp 2	That I thy power may behold		10
	and brightness of thy face,		
	As I have seen thee heretofore	*mf*	11
	within thy holy place.		
m 3	Since better is thy love than life,	V	
	my lips thee praise shall give.		[be
∧ 4	I in thy name will lift my hands,		
	AND BLESS THEE WHILE I LIVE.		
m 5	Ev'n as with marrow and with fat		
	my soul shall filled be;		
mf	THEN SHALL MY MOUTH WITH JOYFUL	*mp*	1
	SING PRAISES UNTO THEE: [LIPS	◊	
m 6	When I do thee upon my bed		
	remember with delight,		
V	And when on thee I meditate		2
	in watches of the night.		
m 7	In shadow of thy wings I'll joy;		
∧	for thou mine help hast been.		
8	My soul thee follows hard; and me		3
	thy right hand doth sustain.		

In whose bent bows are arrows set,
  ev'n sharp and bitter words:
4 That they may at the perfect man
  in secret aim their shot;
  Yea, suddenly they dare at him
  to shoot, and fear it not.

5 In ill encourage they themselves,
  and their snares close do lay:
  Together conference they have;
  Who shall them see? they say.
6 They have search'd out iniquities,
  a perfect search they keep:
  Of each of them the inward thought,
  and very heart, is deep.

mf 7 God shall an arrow shoot at them,
  and wound them suddenly:
8 So their own tongue shall them con-
  all who them see shall fly. [found;
p 9 *And on all men a fear shall fall,*
m   God's works they shall declare;
  For they shall wisely notice take
  what these his doings are.

f 10 IN GOD THE RIGHTEOUS SHALL REJOICE,
  AND TRUST UPON HIS MIGHT;
  YEA, THEY SHALL GREATLY GLORY ALL
  IN HEART THAT ARE UPRIGHT.

mf

p 3

m
Λ

mf

AND WITH THE GOODNESS OF THY HOUSE,
   EV'N OF THY HOLY PLACE.

m 5 O God of our salvation,
      thou, in thy righteousness,
  By fearful works unto our pray'rs
      thine answer dost express:
mf Therefore the ends of all the earth,
      and those afar that be
  Upon the sea, their confidence,
      O Lord, will place in thee.
   6 Who, being girt with pow'r, sets fast
      by his great strength the hills.
   7 Who noise of seas, noise of their waves,
      and people's tumult, stills.
m 8 Those in the utmost parts that dwell
      are at thy signs afraid:
  Th' outgoings of the morn and ev'n
      by thee are joyful made.
mf 9 The earth thou visit'st, wat'ring it;
      thou mak'st it rich to grow
  With God's full flood; thou corn pre-
      when thou provid'st it so.   [par'st,

mf 12

f

    2 SING FORTH THE HONOUR OF HIS NAME,
       AND GLORIOUS MAKE HIS PRAISE.

mp 3 Say unto God, How terrible
      in all thy works art thou!
◊ Through thy great pow'r thy foes to
      shall be constrain'd to bow.   [thee

mf 4 All on the earth shall worship thee,
      they shall thy praise proclaim
∧ In songs: they shall sing cheerfully
      unto thy holy name.

m 5 Come, and the works that God hath
      with admiration see: [wrought
mp   *In's working to the sons of men*
      most terrible is he.

m 6 Into dry land the sea he turu'd,
      and they a passage had;
    Ev'n marching through the flood on
∧   there we in him were glad.   [foot,
mf 7 He ruleth ever by his pow'r;
      his eyes the nations see:
mp   *O let not the rebellious ones*
      lift up themselves on high.

∧

mf 15

17 I with my mouth unto him cry'd,
   my tongue did him extol.

mp 18 *If in my heart I sin regard,*
   the Lord me will not hear:
mf 19 But surely God me heard, and to
   my prayer's voice gave ear.
20 O let the Lord, our gracious God,
   for ever blessed be,
Who turned not my prayer from him,
   nor yet his grace from me.

mf

Λ

mf

Λ

PSALM LXVII.

Narenza 159.   *Prague* 157.

mp 1 LORD, bless and pity us,
   shine on us with thy face:
Λ 2 That th' earth thy way, and nations all
   may know thy saving grace.
mf 3 Let people praise thee, Lord;
   let people all thee praise.
f 4 O LET THE NATIONS BE GLAD,
   IN SONGS THEIR VOICES RAISE:

Another of the same.

Ancona 141.   *Durham* 96

mp

Λ

mf 3

f 4 O LET THE NATIONS BE GLAD,
AND SING FOR JOY ALWAYS

mf For rightly thou shalt people judge,
and nations rule on earth.   [ALL

5 LET PEOPLE PRAISE THEE, LORD; LET
THE FOLK PRAISE THEE WITH MIRTH.

mf 6 Then shall the earth yield her increase;
GOD, OUR GOD, BLESS US SHALL.

7 GOD SHALL US BLESS; AND OF THE
EARTH
THE ENDS SHALL FEAR HIM ALL.

PSALM LXVIII.

Old 68th 33.   *Montrose 49.*

mf 1 LET God arise, and scattered
let all his en'mies be;
And let all those that do him hate
before his presence flee.

2 As smoke is driv'n, so drive thou them;
as fire melts wax away,
Before God's face let wicked men
so perish and decay.

p 8 *Then at God's presence shook the earth,*
    then drops from heaven fell;
    This Sinai shook before the Lord,   14
    the God of Israel.

m 9 O God, thou to thine heritage
    didst send a plenteous rain,   ⋏ 15
    Whereby thou, when it weary was,
    didst it refresh again.

  10 Thy congregation then did make   *mf* 16
    their habitation there:
    Of thine own goodness for the poor,
    O God, thou didst prepare.   17

  11 The Lord himself did give the word,
    the word abroad did spread;
f   Great was the company of them   ⋁
    the same who published.

mf 12 Kings of great armies foiled were.   *f* 18
    and forc'd to flee away;
    And women, who remain'd at home   *ff*
    did distribute the prey.

mp 13 *Though ye have lien among the pots,*   *mf*
mf   like doves ye shall appear,   >

f Yea, ev'n for them, that God the Lord
      in midst of them might dwell.

mf19 Bless'd be the Lord, who is to us
      of our salvation God;
      Who daily with his benefits
      us plenteously doth load.

$\wedge$ 20 He of salvation is the God,
      who is our God most strong;
$\vee$ And unto God the Lord from death
      the issues do belong.

m 21 But surely God shall wound the head
      of those that are his foes;
      The hairy scalp of him that still
      on in his trespass goes.

   22 God said, My people I will bring
      again from Bashan hill;
      Yea, from the sea's devouring depths
      them bring again I will;

   23 That in the blood of enemies
      thy foot imbru'd may be,
      And of thy dogs dipp'd in the same
      the tongues thou mayest see.

:

$\wedge$

m 27

28

$\wedge$ 29

m 30 The spearmen's host, the multitude
　　of bulls, which fiercely look,
　　Those calves which people have forth
Λ　　O Lord our God, rebuke,　　[sent,
　　Till ev'ry one submit himself,
　　and silver pieces bring:
　　The people that delight in war
　　disperse, O God and King.

　 31 Those that be princes great shall then
　　come out of Egypt lands;
Λ　　And Ethiopia to God
　　shall soon stretch out her hands.
mf 32 O all ye kingdoms of the earth,
　　sing praises to this King;
Λ　　FOR HE IS LORD THAT RULETH ALL,
　　UNTO HIM PRAISES SING.

f 33 TO HIM THAT RIDES ON HEAV'NS OF
　　　HEAV'NS,
　　WHICH HE OF OLD DID FOUND;
m　　Lo, he sends out his voice, a voice
Λ　　in might that doth abound.

mf 34 Strength unto God do ye ascribe;
　　for his excellency
Λ　Is over Israel, his strength
　　is in the clouds most high
mp 35 *Thou'rt from thy temple dreadful, Lord;*
mf　　Isr'el's own God is he,
Λ　Who gives his people strength and
　　O LET GOD BLESSED BE.　　[pow'r:

PSALM LXIX.

Ver. 1-21 *Dundee* 144.　　*Silesia* 149.
Ver. 22-29 *Martyrs* 148.　　*St. Nicholas* 151.
Ver. 30-36 *Lancaster* 68.　　*St. Stephen* 62.

mp 1 SAVE me, O God, because the floods
　　do so environ me,
　　That ev'n unto my very soul
　　come in the waters be.
p 2 I downward in deep mire do sink
　　where standing there is none:
　　I am into deep waters come,
　　where floods have o'er me gone.
　 3 I weary with my crying am,
　　my throat is also dry'd;

G

Mine eyes do fail, while for my God
 I waiting do abide.
4 Those men that do without a cause
 bear hatred unto me,
Than are the hairs upon my head
 in number more they be:

They that would me destroy, and are
 mine en'mies wrongfully,
Are mighty: so what I took not,
 to render forc'd was I.
5 Lord, thou my folly know'st, my sins
 not cover'd are from thee.
m 6 Let none that wait on thee be sham'd,
 Lord God of hosts, for me.

O Lord, the God of Israel,
 let none, who search do make,
And seek thee, be at any time
 confounded for my sake.
p 7 For I have borne reproach for thee,
 my face is hid with shame.
8 To brethren strange, to mother's sons
 an alien I became.

V Nor deep me swallow, nor the pit
    her mouth upon me close.

m 16 Hear me, O Lord, because thy love
    and kindness is most good;
    Turn unto me, according to
    thy mercies' multitude.
17 Nor from thy servant hide thy face:
    I'm troubled, soon attend.
18 Draw near my soul, and it redeem;
    me from my foes defend.

p 19 To thee is my reproach well known
    my shame, and my disgrace·
    Those that mine adversaries be
    are all before thy face.
pp 20 *Reproach hath broke my heart; I'm full*
    of grief: I look'd for one
    To pity me, but none I found;
    comforters found I none.

p 21 They also bitter gall did give
    unto me for my meat:
    They gave me vinegar to drink,
    when as my thirst was great.

m 22

23   eyes
    that sight may th
    And let their loins
    co
24 Thy fury pour tho
    and indignation;
    And
mp 25

·26

27

And do not let them come at all
  into thy righteousness.
mp 33

28 Out of the book of life let them
  be raz'd and blotted quite;
f 34

Among the just and righteous
  let not their names be writ.
m 35

p 29 But now become exceeding poor
  and sorrowful am I:

⋀ By thy salvation, O my God
  let me be set on high.
36

mf 30 THE NAME OF GOD I WITH A SONG
  MOST CHEERFULLY WILL PRAISE;
f

AND I, IN GIVING THANKS TO HIM,
  HIS NAME SHALL HIGHLY RAISE.

m 31 This to the Lord a sacrifice
  more gracious shall prove

Than bullock, ox, or any beast
  that hath both horn and hoof.
p 1

32 When this the humble men shall see
  it joy to them shall give:
⋀ 2

O all ye that do seek the Lord,
  your hearts shall ever live.
mp

:

ey, and
that in my hurt delight.

3 Turn'd back be they, Ha, ha! that say,   *mf* 4
   their shaming to requite.

mf 4 IN THEE LET ALL BE GLAD,
    AND JOY THAT SEEK FOR THEE:
    LET THEM WHO THY SALVATION LOVE   *mp*
    SAY STILL, GOD PRAISED BE.
mp 5 I poor and needy am;   ∧
   ∧ come, Lord, and make no stay: ∨
   ∨ MY HELP THOU AND DELIV'RER ART;
     O Lord, make no delay.

Another of the same.

Silesia 149.   St. Mary 145.

p 1 MAKE haste, O God, me to preserve;
     with speed, Lord, succour me.
∧ 2 Let them that for my soul do seek
     sham'd and confounded be:
mp Let them be turned back, and sham'd,
     that in my hurt delight.
·3· Turn'd back be they, Ha, ha! that say,
     their shaming to requite.

∧ Thou gav'st commandment me to save, | 11
FOR THOU'RT MY ROCK AND FORT.

m 4 Free me, my God, from wicked hands, | ∧ 12
hands cruel and unjust:

∧ 5 For thou, O Lord God, art my hope, | 13
AND FROM MY YOUTH MY TRUST.

m 6 Thou from the womb didst hold me up;
thou art the same that me
Out of my mother's bowels took; | ʍ 14
I ever will praise thee.

mp 7 To many I a wonder am; | ∧
but thou'rt my refuge strong.

∧ 8 Fill'd let my mouth be with thy praise | f 15
and honour all day long.

mp 9 O do not cast me off, when as | ∨
old age doth overtake me ;
And when my strength decayed is, | mf 16
then do not thou forsake me.

m 10 For those that are mine enemies
against me speak with hate;
And they together counsel take | m 17
that for my soul lay wait.

And hitherto I have declar'd
the wonders thou hast wrought.

p 18 *And now, Lord, leave me not, when I*
old and gray-headed grow:

Till to this age thy strength and pow'r
to all to come I show.

mf 19 And thy most perfect righteousness,
O Lord, is very high,
Who hast so great things done: O God,
who is like unto thee?

mp 20 Thou, Lord, who great adversities,
and sore, to me didst show,
Shalt quicken, and bring me again
from depths of earth below.

mf 21 My greatness and my pow'r thou wilt
increase, and far extend:
On ev'ry side against all grief
thou wilt me comfort send.

22 Thee, ev'n thy truth, I'll also praise,
my God, with psaltery:
THOU HOLY ONE OF ISRAEL,
WITH HARP I'LL SING TO THEE.

23 MY LIPS SHALL MUCH REJOICE IN THEE,
WHEN I THY PRAISES SOUND;
MY SOUL, WHICH THOU REDEEMED HAST,
IN JOY SHALL MUCH ABOUND.

mf 24 My tongue thy justice shall proclaim,
continuing all day long;
For they confounded are, and sham'd,
that seek to do me wrong.

mp 4

f   AND THOSE SHALL HE IN PIECES BREAK   *f* 11
      WHO THEM OPPRESSED HAVE.

m 5 They shall thee fear, while sun and
      do last, through ages all.   [moon
mp 6 Like rain on mown grass he shall drop,
      or show'rs on earth that fall.

m 7 The just shall flourish in his days,
      and prosper in his reign:
      He shall, while doth the moon endure,
      abundant peace maintain.
mf 8 His large and great dominion shall
      from sea to sea extend:
      It from the river shall reach forth
      unto earth's utmost end.

    9 They in the wilderness that dwell
      bow down before him must;
      And they that are his enemies
      shall lick the very dust.
  10 The kings of Tarshish, and the isles,
      to him shall presents bring;
      And unto him shall offer gifts
      Sheba's and Seba's king.

With prosp'rous fruit shall shake, like   *m*
  on Lebanon that be.   [trees

The city shall be flourishing,
  her citizens abound
In number shall, like to the grass   *mp* 3
  that grows upon the ground.
mf 17 His name for ever shall endure;
  last like the sun it shall:
Men shall be bless'd in him, and bless'd   *m*
  all nations shall him call.

 18 Now blessed be the Lord our God,
  the God of Israel,
For he alone doth wondrous works,
  in glory that excel.
f 19 AND BLESSED BE HIS GLORIOUS NAME
  TO ALL ETERNITY:
ff THE WHOLE EARTH LET HIS GLORY FILL.
  AMEN, SO LET IT BE.

PSALM LXXIII.

Ver. 1-22 *St. Paul* 50.   *St. James* 98.
Ver. 23-28 *St. Lawrence* 96   *Brunswick* 101

And their reproaching tongue through- 15
   the earth at large doth walk.   [out   to

mp 10 His people oftentimes for this
   look back, and turn about·
Sith waters of so full a cup   *mp* 16
   to these are poured out.

m 11 And thus they say, How can it be   17
   that God these things doth know?
Or, Can there in the Highest be   *p* 18
   knowledge of things below?   *a*   *ry p*
                                         denly

12 Behold, these are the wicked ones
   yet prosper at their will
In worldly things; they do increase   *m* 19
   in wealth and riches still.   they!
13 I verily have done in vain   *utterly*
   my heart to purify;
To no effect in innocence   20
   washed my hands have I.

14 For daily, and all day throughout,
   great plagues I suffer'd have;
Yea, ev'ry morning I of new   *m* 21
   did chastisement receive.   :

mp 22 So rude was I, and ignorant,
    and in thy sight a beast.
  23 Nevertheless continually,
    O Lord, I am with thee:
    Thou dost me hold by my right hand,
    and still upholdest me.

m 24 Thou, with thy counsel, while I live,
    wilt me conduct and guide;
    And to thy glory afterward
    receive me to abide.
  25 Whom have I in the heavens high
    but thee, O Lord, alone?
    And in the earth whom I desire
    besides thee there is none.

p 26 *My flesh and heart doth faint and fail,*
mf   but God doth fail me never:
    For of my heart God is the strength
    and portion for ever.
mp 27 For, lo, they that are far from thee
    for ever perish shall;
    Them that a whoring from thee go
    thou hast destroyed all.

m 28 But surely it is good for me
    that I draw near to God:
    IN GOD I TRUST, THAT ALL THY WORKS
    I MAY DECLARE ABROAD.

p 1

     For all the ills thy foes have done
       within thy sanctuary.

  4 Amidst thy congregations
     thine enemies do roar:
   Their ensigns they set up for signs
     of triumph thee before.

m 5 A man was famous, and was had
     in estimation,
   According as he lifted up
     his axe thick trees upon.

p 6 But all at once with axes now
     and hammers they go to,
   And down the carved work thereof
     they break, and quite undo.

  7 They fired have thy sanctuary,
     and have defil'd the same,
   By casting down unto the ground
     the place where dwelt thy name.

  8 Thus said they in their hearts, Let us
     destroy them out of hand:
   They burnt up all the synagogues
     of God within the land.

manifold.

Him to be meat unto the folk
  in wilderness that live.
15 Thou clav'st the fountain and the flood,
  which did with streams abound:
  Thou dry'dst the mighty waters up
  unto the very ground.

16 Thine only is the day, O Lord,
  thine also is the night;
  And thou alone prepared hast
  the sun and shining light.

17 By thee the borders of the earth
  were settled ev'ry where:
  The summer and the winter both
  by thee created were.

mp 18 That th' enemy reproached hath,
  O keep it in record;
  And that the foolish people have
  blasphem'd thy name, O Lord.

19 Unto the multitude do not
  thy turtle's soul deliver:
  The congregation of thy poor
  do not forget for ever.

20 Unto thy cov'nant have respect;
  for earth's dark places be
  Full of the habitations
  of horrid cruelty.

m 21 O let not those that be oppress'd
  return again with shame:
  Let those that poor and needy are
  give praise unto thy name.

22 Do thou, O God, arise and plead
  the cause that is thine own:
  Remember how thou art reproach'd
  still by the foolish one.

23 Do not forget the voice of those
  that are thine enemies:
  Of those the tumult ever grows
  that do against thee rise.

PSALM LXXV.
Bethel 89.   *St. Andrew 72.*

mf 1 TO thee, O God, do we give thanks
  we do give thanks to thee·
  Because thy'wondrous works declare
  thy great name near to be.

m 2 I purpose, when I shall receive
  the congregation,
  That I shall judgment uprightly
  render to ev'ry one.

p 3 Dissolved is the land, with all
  that in the same do dwell;
  But I the pillars thereof do
∧ bear up, and stablish well.

m 4 I to the foolish people said,
  Do not deal foolishly;
  And unto those that wicked are,
  Lift not your horn on high.

 5 Lift not your horn on high, nor speak
 6 with stubborn neck. But know,
  That not from east, nor west, nor south,
  promotion doth flow.

mf 7 But God is judge; he puts down one,
  and sets another up.

mp 8 For in the hand of God most high
  of red wine is a cup:

  'Tis full of mixture, he pours forth,
∧ and makes the wicked all

  Wring out the bitter dregs thereof;
mf yea, and they drink them shall.
f 9 But I for ever will declare,
  I Jacob's God will praise.
 10 All horns of lewd men I'll cut off;
  but just men's horns will raise.

f

∧

m
p
m

    Their horses and their chariots both
      were in a dead sleep cast.

m 7 Thou, Lord, ev'n thou art he that should
      be fear'd; and who is he
   That may stand up before thy sight,   *m*
      if once thou angry be?

    8 From heav'n thou judgment caus'd be
p   *the earth was still with fear,* [heard;
m 9 When God to judgment rose, to save   *p*
   all meek on earth that were.

  10 Surely the very wrath of man
    unto thy praise redounds:
   Thou to the remnant of his wrath
    wilt set restraining bounds.
*mf*11 Vow to the Lord your God, and pay:
    all ye that near him be,
   Bring gifts and presents unto him;   4
p   *for to be fear'd is he.*

m 12 By him the sp'rits shall be cut off   *pp*
   of those that princes are:
   Unto the kings that are on earth   *mp* 5
    he fearful doth appear.

The times and ages that are past   *m* 12
    full many years agone.
6 By night my song I call to mind,
    and commune with my heart;
My sp'rit did carefully enquire   *mp* 13
    how I might ease my smart.

p 7 For ever will the Lord cast off,
    and gracious be no more?
8 For ever is his mercy gone?   *mf* 14
    fails his word evermore?
9 Is't true that to be gracious
    the Lord forgotten hath?
And that his tender mercies he   15
    hath shut up in his wrath?

m 10 Then did I say, That surely this
    is mine infirmity:
I'LL MIND THE YEARS OF THE RIGHT   16
    OF HIM THAT IS MOST HIGH. [HAND
11 YEA, I REMEMBER WILL THE WORKS   *p*
    PERFORMED BY THE LORD:
THE WONDERS DONE OF OLD BY THEE   *mf* 17
    I SURELY WILL RECORD.

And swiftly through the world abroad
thine arrows fierce did fly.

f 18 THY THUNDER'S VOICE ALONGST THE
A MIGHTY NOISE DID MAKE; [HEAV'N
BY LIGHTNINGS LIGHTEN'D WAS THE
WORLD,
p   th' earth tremble did and shake.
m 19 Thy way is in the sea, and in
the waters great thy path
mp Yet are thy footsteps hid, O Lord;
none knowledge thereof hath.

m 20 Thy people thou didst safely lead,
like to a flock of sheep;
By Moses' hand and Aaron's thou
didst them conduct and keep.

PSALM LXXVIII.
Stafford 94.   *Tallis 93.*

m 1 ATTEND, my people, to my law;
thereto give thou an ear;
The words that from my mouth proceed
attentively do hear.

2   spe
      and sayings dark

3

4

mf   The

f

m 5

6

7

H

In right - eous - ness to judge the world, Jus - tice to give each one.

'Gainst Jacob, and 'gainst Israel   29
    up indignation came.

22 For they believ'd not God, nor trust
    in his salvation had;
m 23 Though clouds above he did command,   *mp* 30
    and heav'n's doors open made,
24 And manna rain'd on them, and gave
    them corn of heav'n to eat.
25 Man angels' food did eat; to them   31
    he to the full sent meat.

26 And in the heaven he did cause
    an eastern wind to blow;
And by his power he let out   32
    the southern wind to go.
mf 27 Then flesh as thick as dust he made   And
    to rain down them among;
And feather'd fowls, like as the sand   *p* 33
    which li'th the shore along.

28 At his command amidst their camp
    these show'rs of flesh down fell,
All round about the tabernacles   *mp* 34
    and tents where they did dwell.

Yea, they return'd, and after God
right early did enquire.

m 35 And that the Lord had been their Rock,
they did remember then;
Ev'n that the high almighty God
had their Redeemer been.

mp 36 Yet with their mouth they flatter'd him,
and spake but feignedly
And they unto the God of truth
with their false tongues did lie.

37 For though their words were good, their
with him was not sincere;   [heart
Unstedfast and perfidious
they in his cov'nant were.

38 But, full of pity, he forgave
their sin, them did not slay;
Nor stirr'd up all his wrath, but oft
his anger turn'd away.

39 For that they were but fading flesh
to mind he did recall;
A wind that passeth soon away
and not returns at all.

40

41

m 42

43 Nor
he o

44

45

e

     And divers kinds of filthy frogs   *mf* 52
       he sent them to destroy.

46 He to the caterpillar gave
   the fruits of all their soil;
  Their labours he deliver'd up   53
    unto the locusts' spoil.
mf 47 Their vines with hail, their sycamores
   he with the frost did blast:
48 Their beasts to hail he gave; their flocks   54 .
   hot thunderbolts did waste.

49 Fierce burning wrath he on them cast,
   and indignation strong,
  And troubles sore, by sending forth   55
    ill angels them among.
50 He to his wrath made way; their soul   B
   from death he did not save·
  But over to the pestilence
    the lives of them he gave.

mp 51 In Egypt land the first-born all
   he smote down ev'ry where;
  Among the tents of Ham, ev'n these   *mp* 56
    chief of their strength that were.

And to observe his testimonies
did not incline their will:
57 But, like their fathers, turned back,
and dealt unfaithfully:
Aside they turned, like a bow   *f* 65
that shoots deceitfully.

58 For they to anger did provoke
him with their places high;
And with their graven images   .
mov'd him to jealousy.   66
59 When God heard this, he waxed wroth,
and much loath'd Isr'el then:
60 So Shiloh's tent he left, the tent   *m* 67
which he had plac'd with men.

61 And he his strength delivered
into captivity;
He left his glory in the hand   68
of his proud enemy.
62 His people also he gave o'er
unto the sword's fierce rage:
So sore his wrath inflamed was   *mf* 69
against his heritage.

Like to the earth which he did found
  to perpetuity.

m 70 Of David, that his servant was,
    he also choice did make,
  And even from the folds of sheep
    was pleased him to take:

71 From waiting on the ewes with young,
    he brought him forth to feed
  Israel, his inheritance,
    his people, Jacob's seed.

72 So after the integrity
    he of his heart them fed;
  And by the good skill of his hands
    them wisely governed.

PSALM LXXIX.

Martyrs 148.   *Crowle* 153.

p 1 O GOD, the heathen enter'd have
    thine heritage; by them
  Defiled is thy house: on heaps
    they laid Jerusalem.

2 The bodies of thy servants they
    have cast forth to be meat
  To rav'nous fowls; thy dear saints'
    they gave to beasts to eat.   [flesh

3 Their blood about Jerusalem
    like water they have shed;
  And there was none to bury them
    when they were slain and dead.

p 4 Unto our neighbours a reproach
    most base become are we;
  A scorn and laughingstock to them
    that round about us be.

mp 5 How long, Lord, shall thine anger last?
    wilt thou still keep the same?
  And shall thy fervent jealousy
    burn like unto a flame?

mf 6 On heathen pour thy fury forth,
    that have thee never known,
  And on those kingdoms which thy name
    have never call'd upon.

7 For these are they who Jacob have
    devoured cruelly;

V	And they his habitation have caused waste to lie.		*m* 13		epherd! like a flock
mp 8	Against us mind not former sins; thy tender mercies show;		∧		Joseph guide;
V	Let them prevent us speedily, for we're brought very low.				ou that dost between
m 9	For thy name's glory help us, Lord who hast our Saviour been:		*mp* 1		
V	Deliver us; for thy name's sake, O purge away our sin.		∧		

mf 10	Why say the heathen, Where's their
	  let him to them be known; [God?
	 When those who shed thy servants'
	  are in our sight o'erthrown. [blood
			m 2
			 ∧		

mp 11
 ∧
 V
	O let the pris'ner's sighs ascend
	  before thy sight on high;
	 Preserve those in thy mighty pow'r
	  that are design'd to die.
			mp 3
			 ∧		

12	And to our neighbours' bosom cause
	  it sev'n-fold render'd be,
	 Ev'n the reproach wherewith they have,
	  O Lord, reproached thee.
			p 4		e

pp 5 *Thou tears of sorrow giv'st to them*
    instead of bread to eat;
  Yea, tears instead of drink thou giv'st   11
    to them in measure great.
  6 *Thou makest us a strife unto ·*
    our neighbours round about ·
  Our enemies among themselves   *p* 12
    at us do laugh and flout.

p 7 Turn us again, O God of hosts
    and upon us vouchsafe
∧ To make thy countenance to shine   13
    and so we shall be safe.
m 8 A vine from Egypt brought thou hast,
    by thine outstretched hand;
  And thou the heathen out didst cast,   *mp* 14
    to plant it in their land.

  9 Before it thou a room didst make,   ∧
    where it might grow and stand;
  Thou causedst it deep root to take,   15
    and it did fill the land
10 The mountains vail'd were with its shade,
    as with a covering;

p 16 Burnt up it is with flaming fire,
    it also is cut down:
  They utterly are perished,
    when as thy face doth frown.

m 17 O let thy hand be still upon
    the Man of thy right hand,
  The Son of man, whom for thyself
    thou madest strong to stand.
mf 18 So henceforth we will not go back,
    nor turn from thee at all:
m   O do thou quicken us, and we
    upon thy name will call.

19 Turn us again, Lord God of hosts,
    and upon us vouchsafe
  To make thy countenance to shine,
    AND SO WE SHALL BE SAFE.

PSALM LXXXI.

Old 81st 34.   *New London 53.*

f 1 SING loud to God our strength; with
    to Jacob's God do sing.   [joy

2

3

4

m 5

7
mf
m

9 In midst of thee there shall not be
   any strange god at all;
   Nor unto any god unknown
    thou bowing down shalt fall.
*mf*10 I am the Lord thy God, which did
   from Egypt land thee guide·
f I'll fill thy mouth abundantly
   do thou it open wide.

16

p 11 *But yet my people to my voice*
   would not attentive be;
   And ev'n my chosen Israel
   he would have none of me.
12 *So to the lust of their own hearts*
   I them delivered; ·
   And then in counsels of their own
   they vainly wandered.
*mp*13 O that my people had me heard,
   Isr'el my ways had chose!
*mf*14 I had their en'mies soon subdu'd
   my hand turn'd on their foes.
15 The haters of the Lord to him
   submission should have feign'd;

PSALM LXXXII.

St. James 93   St. Thomas 75

mf 1

m 2

3

4

p 5

:

m 6 I said that ye are gods, and are
    sons of the Highest all:
p 7 *But ye shall die like men, and as*
    one of the princes fall.

                                 4

f 8 O GOD, DO THOU RAISE UP THYSELF
    THE EARTH TO JUDGMENT CALL:
    FOR THOU, AS THINE INHERITANCE,   5
    SHALT TAKE THE NATIONS ALL.

                                 6   e.

PSALM LXXXIII.

Coleshill 146.   *St. Nicholas 151.*

                                 7

mf 1 KEEP not, O God, we thee entreat,   8
      O keep not silence now:
    Do thou not hold thy peace, O God,
      and still no more be thou.   *mf* 9
    2 For, lo, thine enemies a noise
      tumultuously have made;   10
    And they that haters are of thee   as
      have lifted up the head.   11

m 3 Against thy chosen people they
    do crafty counsel take;

12 Who said, For our possession   *p* 2
     let us God's houses take.   y

13 My God, them like a wheel, as chaff   *mf*
     before the wind, them make.

14 As fire consumes the wood, as flame   *mp* 3
     doth mountains set on fire,

15 Chase and affright them with the storm
     and tempest of thine ire.

mp 16 Their faces fill with shame, O Lord,   *m*
     that they may seek thy name.

⋀ 17 Let them confounded be, and vex'd,   *mf*
     and perish in their shame:

mf 18 That men may know that thou, to whom   4
     alone doth appertain

⋀   The name JEHOVAH, dost most high
     o'er all the earth remain.   5

PSALM LXXXIV.

Manchester 70.   *University 107.*

mp 1 HOW lovely is thy dwelling-place,   *mp* 6
     O Lord of hosts, to me!
     The tabernacles of thy grace
     how pleasant, Lord, they be!

7 So they from strength unwearied go
   still forward unto strength
   Until in Sion they appear
   before the Lord at length.

p 8 Lord God of hosts, my prayer hear;
   O Jacob's God, give ear.

9 See God our shield, look on the face
   of thine anointed dear.

m 10 For in thy courts one day excels
   a thousand; rather in
   My God's house will I keep a door
   than dwell in tents of sin.

f 11 FOR GOD THE LORD'S A SUN AND SHIELD:
   HE'LL GRACE AND GLORY GIVE;
   AND WILL WITHOLD NO GOOD FROM THEM
   THAT UPRIGHTLY DO LIVE.

m 12 O thou that art the Lord of hosts,
   that man is truly blest,
   Who by assured confidence
   on thee alone doth rest.

m 1   :

2   all   thy iniquities;

3

4

p 5

m 6

7

8 I'll hear what God the Lord will speak:
   to his folk he'll speak peace,
And to his saints; but let them not
   return to foolishness.

mp

9 To them that fear him surely near
   is his salvation;
That glory in our land may have
   her habitation.

mp 3

mf 10 Truth met with mercy, righteousness
   and peace kiss'd mutually: [eousness

4

11 Truth springs from earth, and right-
   looks down from heaven high.

m 5

f 12 YEA, WHAT IS GOOD THE LORD SHALL
   GIVE;
OUR LAND SHALL YIELD INCREASE:

6

13 JUSTICE, TO SET US IN HIS STEPS,
   SHALL GO BEFORE HIS FACE.

7

PSALM LXXXVI.

Ver. 1.7 *Evan* 125.   St. *Mary* 145.
Ver. 8-13 St. *Ann* 60.   *New London* 53.
Ver. 14-17 St. *Chad* 152.   *Walsal* 155.

mf 8

p 1 *O LORD, do thou bow down thine ear,*
   and hear me graciously;

are·

PSALM LXXXVI.

m 9 All nations whom thou mad'st shall come
    and worship rev'rently
  Before thy face; and they, O Lord,
    thy name shall glorify.
mf 10 Because thou art exceeding great,
    and works by thee are done
  Which are to be admir'd; and thou
    art God thyself alone.

mp 11 Teach me thy way, and in thy truth
    O Lord, then walk will I;
  Unite my heart, that I thy name
    may fear continually.
f 12 O LORD MY GOD, WITH ALL MY HEART
    TO THEE I WILL GIVE PRAISE;
  AND I THE GLORY WILL ASCRIBE
    UNTO THY NAME ALWAYS:

  13 BECAUSE THY MERCY TOWARD ME
    IN GREATNESS DOTH EXCEL;
  AND THOU DELIVER'D HAST MY SOUL
    out from the lowest hell.
mp 14 O God, the proud against me rise,
    and vi'lent men have met,

before		
15		
16		
∧		son
m 17		
m 1		
∧ 2		all,

f 3 Things glorious are said of thee,
   thou city of the Lord.
m 4 Rahab and Babel I, to those
   that know me, will record:

   Behold ev'n Tyrus, and with it
    the land of Palestine
   And likewise Ethiopia;
    this man was born therein.
mf 5 And it of Sion shall be said,
    This man and that man there
   Was born; and he that is most High
    himself shall stablish her.

f 6 When God the people writes, he'll
    count
   That this man born was there.
  7 There be that sing and play; and
    all
  My well-springs in thee are.

PSALM LXXXVIII.
Bangor 147. *Crowle* 153.

pp 1 LORD God, my Saviour, day and
   before thee cry'd have I. [night

2

3

4

5

6
  in

7

8

9
  mine   :

mp 10 ·Wilt thou shew wonders to the dead?
  shall they rise, and thee bless?
 11 Shall in the grave thy love be told?
  in death thy faithfulness?
 12 Shall thy great wonders in the dark
  or shall thy righteousness·
  Be known to any in the land
  of deep forgetfulness?

m 13 But, Lord, to thee I cry'd; my pray'r
  at morn prevent shall thee.
 14 Why, Lord, dost thou cast off my soul,
  and hid'st thy face from me?
p 15 Distress'd am I, and from my youth
  I ready am to die;
  Thy terrors I have borne, and am
  distracted fearfully.

 16 The dreadful fierceness of thy wrath
  quite over me doth go:
  Thy terrors great have cut me off,
  they did pursue me so. .
 17 For round about me ev'ry day,
  like water, they did roll;

pp 18

f 1

mf 2

m 3

And to my servant, whom I lov'd,
  to David sworn have I·

mf 4 That I thy seed establish shall
  for ever to remain,
And will to generations all
  thy throne build and maintain.

f 5 THE PRAISES OF THY WONDERS, LORD,
  THE HEAVENS SHALL EXPRESS·
AND IN THE CONGREGATION
  OF SAINTS THY FAITHFULNESS.

mf 6 For who in heaven with the Lord
  may once himself compare?
Who is like God among the sons
  of those that mighty are?

mp 7 Great fear in meeting of the saints
  is due unto the Lord;
And he of all about him should
  with rev'rence be ador'd.

mf 8 O thou that art the Lord of hosts
  what Lord in mightiness
Is like to thee? who compass'd round
  art with thy faithfulness.

9

∧
∨

mf 10

And with

11

12

f 13

<

m 14 Justice and judgment of thy throne
    are made the dwelling-place;
  Mercy, accompany'd with truth,   20
    shall go before thy face.

*mf*15 O greatly bless'd the people are
    the joyful sound that know;
  In brightness of thy face, O Lord   *mf*21
    they ever on shall go.
 16 They in thy name shall all the day   22
    rejoice exceedingly;
  And in thy righteousness shall they   23
    exalted be on high.

 17 Because the glory of their strength
    doth only stand in thee;
  And in thy favour shall our horn   24
    and pow'r exalted be.
 18 For God is our defence; and he
    to us doth safety bring: ∧
  The Holy One of Israel   *mf*25
    is our almighty King.
m 19 In vision to thy Holy One   ∧
    thou saidst, I help upon

PSALM LXXXIX.

m 26 Thou art my Father, he shall cry,
    thou art my God alone;
    And he shall say, **Thou art the Rock**
    of my salvation.
*mf*27 I'll make him my first-**born more high**
    than kings of any land.
   28 My love I'll ever keep **for him**
    my cov'nant fast shall stand.

   29 His seed I by my pow'r **will make**
    for ever to endure;
    And, as the days of heav'n, his throne
    shall stable be, and sure.
p 30 *But if his children shall forsake*
    my laws, and go astray,
    And in my judgments shall not walk
    but wander from my way :

*mp*31 If they my laws break, and do not
    keep my commandements;
   32 I'll visit then their faults with rods
    their sins with chastisements.
m 33 Yet I'll not take my love from him,
    nor false my promise make.

34

35
*mf*36

37

p 38

39

40

41

sse
to n

42 *Thou hast set up his foes' right hand;*
   mad'st all his en'mies glad:
43 *Turn'd his sword's edge, and him to stand*   50
   in battle hast not made.

44 *His glory thou hast made to cease,*
   his throne to ground down cast;
45 *Shorten'd his days of youth, and him*   51
   with shame thou cover'd hast.

mp 46 How long, Lord, wilt thou hide thyself?
   for ever, in thine ire?
   And shall thine indignation   *mf* 52
   burn like unto a fire?

47 Remember, Lord, how short a time
   I shall on earth remain:
   O wherefore is it so that thou
   hast made all men in vain?
48 What man is he that liveth here
   and death shall never see?
   Or from the power of the grave   *m* 1
   what man his soul shall free?
49 Thy former loving-kindnesses,   2
   O Lord, where be they now?

[p
all,

:

Ere ever thou hadst form'd the earth,
  and all the world abroad;
Ev'n thou from everlasting art
  to everlasting God.

∧

p 3 *Thou dost unto destruction*
  man that is mortal turn;
mp And unto them thou say'st, Again,   10
  ye sons of men, return.
  4 Because a thousand years appear
    no more before thy sight
  Than yesterday, when it is past,
    or than a watch by night.

  5 As with an overflowing flood
    thou carry'st them away:

∨ They like a sleep are, like the grass   11
    that grows at morn are they.
  6 At morn it flourishes and grows,   12
    cut down at ev'n doth fade.
p 7 *For by thine anger we're consum'd,*
∨   *thy wrath makes us afraid.*
mp 8 Our sins thou and iniquities
  dost in thy presence place,

:

m 13 Turn yet again to us, O Lord
    how long thus shall it be?
    Let it repent thee now for those   *mp* 1
    that servants are to thee.
  14 O with thy tender mercies, Lord
    us early satisfy;
    So we rejoice shall all our days,   *m* 2
    and still be glad in thee.

mp 15 According as the days have been,
    wherein we grief have had,
    And years wherein we ill have seen   *m* 3
    so do thou make us glad.
m 16 O let thy work and pow'r appear
    thy servants' face before
    And shew unto their children dear   4
    thy glory evermore:

f 17 AND LET THE BEAUTY OF THE LORD
    OUR GOD BE US UPON:
    OUR HANDY-WORKS ESTABLISH THOU   *mp* 5
    ESTABLISH THEM EACH ONE.

6 Nor for the pestilence, that walks
  in darkness secretly;
⋀ Nor for destruction, that doth waste   *mf* 13
  at noon-day openly.

7 A thousand at thy side shall fall,
  on thy right hand shall lie
  Ten thousand dead; yet unto thee   14
  it shall not once come nigh.
m 8 Only thou with thine eyes shalt look
  and a beholder be;
  And thou therein the just reward
  of wicked men shalt see.

9 Because the Lord, who constantly
  my refuge is alone,
  Ev'n the most High, is made by thee   *mf* 16   unto his mind
  thy habitation;   I will him   ;
10 No plague shall near thy dwelling come;
  no ill shall thee befall:
11 For thee to keep in all thy ways
  his angels charge he shall.
12 They in their hands shall bear thee up,
  still waiting thee upon:

PSALM XCII

mf 1 To render thanks unto the Lord
     it is a comely thing,
     And to thy name, O thou most High,
     due praise aloud to sing.
   2 Thy loving-kindness to shew forth   *mf* 8
     when shines the morning light;
     And to declare thy faithfulness   *mp* 9
     with pleasure ev'ry night,

   3 On a ten-stringed instrument,
     upon the psaltery,
     And on the harp with solemn sound,   *f* 10
∨   and grave sweet melody.
mf 4 For thou, Lord, by thy mighty works
     hast made my heart right glad;
∧   And I will triumph in the works   *m* 11
     which by thine hands were made.

mp 5 How great, Lord, are thy works! each
     of thine a deep it is: [thought
   6 A brutish man it knoweth not;   12
     fools understand not this.
   7 When those that lewd and wicked are
     spring quickly up like grass,

13 Those that within the house of God
  are planted by his grace,
They shall grow up, and flourish all
  in our God's holy place.

14 And in old age, when others fade,
  they fruit still forth shall bring;
They shall be fat, and full of sap,
  and aye be flourishing;
15 To shew that upright is the Lord:
  he is a rock to me,
And he from all unrighteousness
  is altogether free.

PSALM XCIII.

Montrose 49. *Old 29th 31.*

mf 1 THE Lord doth reign, and cloth'd is he
  with majesty most bright;
His works do shew him cloth'd to be,
  and girt about with might.
m The world is also stablished,
  that it cannot depart.

2 Lift up thyself, thou of the earth
   the sov'reign Judge that art;
And unto those that are so proud   10
   a due reward impart.

mp 3 How long, O mighty God, shall they
     who lewd and wicked be,
  How long shall they who wicked are   *mp* 11
     thus triumph haughtily?
  4 How long shall things most hard by   12
     be uttered and told?   [them
  And all that work iniquity   13
     to boast themselves be bold?

p 5 *Thy folk they break in pieces, Lord,*
     thine heritage oppress:
  6 *The widow they and stranger slay,*   *m* 14
     and kill the fatherless.
mp 7 Yet say they, God it shall not see,
     nor God of Jacob know.
  8 Ye brutish people! understand;   15
     fools! when wise will ye grow?

m 9 The Lord did plant the ear of man,
     and hear then shall not he?

16 Who will rise up for me against
those that do wickedly?
Who will stand up for me 'gainst those
that work iniquity?
17 Unless the Lord had been my help
when I was sore opprest,
p   *Almost my soul had in the house*
of silence been at rest.

*mp*18 When I had uttered this word,
>   (my foot doth slip away,)
ui   Thy mercy held me up, O Lord,
thy goodness did me stay.
19 Amidst the multitude of thoughts
which in my heart do fight,
My soul, lest it be overcharg'd,
thy comforts do delight.

20 Shall of iniquity the throne
have fellowship with thee,
Which mischief, cunningly contriv'd,
doth by a law decree?
*mp*21 Against the righteous souls they join,
they guiltless blood condemn.

mf 22 But of my refuge God's the rock,
and my defence from them.

m 23 On them their own iniquity
the Lord shall bring and lay,
And cut them off in their own sin;
our Lord God shall them slay.

PSALM XCV.

Durham 95.   *Tallis* 93.

mf

$\wedge$
f

4

5 To him the spacious sea belongs,
   for he the same did make;
The dry land also from his hands
   its form at first did take.

mp 6 *O come, and let us worship him,*
     let us bow down withal,
   And on our knees before the Lord
     our Maker let us fall.
m 7 For he's our God, the people we
   of his own pasture are,
And of his hand the sheep; to-day,
   if ye his voice will hear,

mp 8 *Then harden not your hearts, as in*
     the provocation,
   As in the desert, on the day
     of the tentation:
9 *When me your fathers tempt'd and prov'd,*
   and did my working see;
10 *Ev'n for the space of forty years*
   this race hath grieved me.

   I said, This people errs in heart,
     my ways they do not know:

11 *To whom I sware in wrath, that to*
     my rest they should not go.

PSALM XCVI.

St. Magnus 45.   *Colchester 111.*

mf   :

mp 5

f

6 Great honour is before his face,
  and majesty divine;
  Strength is within his holy place,
  and there doth beauty shine.

m 7 Do ye ascribe unto the Lord,
  of people ev'ry tribe,
  Glory do ye unto the Lord,
  and mighty pow'r ascribe.

8 Give ye the glory to the Lord
  that to his name is due;
  Come ye into his courts, and bring
  an offering with you.

9 In beauty of his holiness,
  O do the Lord adore;

mp Likewise let all the earth throughout
  tremble his face before.

*mf*10 Among the heathen say, God reigns;
  the world shall stedfastly
  Be fix'd from moving; he shall judge
  the people righteously.

f 11 Let heav'ns be glad before the Lord,
  and let the earth rejoice;

Let seas, and all that is therein,
  cry out, and make a noise.

12 Let fields rejoice, and ev'ry thing
  that springeth of the earth:
  Then woods and ev'ry tree shall sing
  with gladness and with mirth

m 13 Before the Lord; because he comes,
  to judge the earth comes he:
  He'll judge the world with righteous-
  the people faithfully.   [ness,

PSALM XCVII.

Old 29th 31.   *Palestrina 92.*

f 1 GOD reigneth, let the earth be glad,
  and isles rejoice each one.

mp 2 Dark clouds him compass; and in right
  with judgment dwells his throne.

mf 3 Fire goes before him, and his foes
  it burns up round about:

4 His lightnings lighten did the world;
  earth saw, and shook throughout.

m 5 Hills at the presence of the Lord,
    like wax, did melt away;
∧   Ev'n at the presence of the Lord
    of all the earth, I say.
mf 6 The heav'ns declare his righteousness,
    all men his glory see.
  7 All who serve graven images,
    confounded let them be.

    Who do of idols boast themselves
    let shame upon them fall:
mp   *Ye that are called gods, see that*
    ye do him worship all.
f 8 Sion did hear, and joyful was,
    glad Judah's daughters were;
    They much rejoic'd, O Lord, because
    thy judgments did appear.

  9 For thou, O Lord, art high above
    all things on earth that are·
    Above all other gods thou art
    exalted very far.
m 10 Hate ill, all ye that love the Lord:
    his saints' souls keepeth he;

∧
m 11
∧
mf 12

PSALM XCVIII.

Liverpool 69.   *Bedford* 61.

f 1

    :

2

m 3 He mindful of his grace and truth
      to Isr'el's house hath been;
      And the salvation of our God
      all ends of th' earth have seen.
f 4 Let all the earth unto the Lord
      send forth a joyful noise;
      LIFT UP YOUR VOICE ALOUD TO HIM,
      SING PRAISES, AND REJOICE.

f 5 With harp, with harp, and voice of
      unto JEHOVAH sing: [psalms,
   6 WITH TRUMPETS, CORNETS, GLADLY
         SOUND
      BEFORE THE LORD THE KING.
   7 LET SEAS AND ALL THEIR FULNESS
         ROAR;
      THE WORLD, AND DWELLERS THERE;
   8 LET FLOODS CLAP HANDS, AND LET THE
      TOGETHER JOY DECLARE   [HILLS

m 9 BEFORE THE LORD; because he comes,
      to judge the earth comes he:
      He'll judge the world with righteous-
      his folk with equity.   [ness,

m	
p	
m	
p	
m	2
	:
mf	5
mp	
<>	:
m	6

K

m 7 Within the pillar of the cloud
    he unto them did speak:
    The testimonies he them taught
    and laws, they did not break.

   8 Thou answer'dst them, O Lord our God;
    thou wast a God that gave
    Pardon to them, though on their deeds
    thou wouldest vengeance have.
mf 9 Do ye exalt the Lord our God,
    and at his holy hill
    Do ye him worship: for the Lord
    our God is holy still.

PSALM C.
Old Hundred 1.

mf 1 ALL people that on earth do dwell,
    Sing to the Lord with cheerful voice.
   2 Him serve with mirth, his praise forth
    tell,
    Come ye before him and rejoice.
m 3 Know that the Lord is God indeed;
    Without our aid he did us make:

f 4

m 5

mf

m

f   4 ENTER HIS GATES AND COURTS WITH
      PRAISE,
      TO THANK HIM GO YE THITHER:
      TO HIM EXPRESS YOUR THANKFULNESS,
      AND BLESS HIS NAME TOGETHER.
m   5 Because the Lord our God is good,
      his mercy faileth never;
      And to all generations
f   HIS TRUTH ENDURETH EVER.

PSALM CI.

Chester 154.   *Lancaster 68.*

m   1 I MERCY will and judgment sing,
      Lord, I will sing to thee.
    2 With wisdom in a perfect way
      shall my behaviour be.
mp   O when, in kindness unto me,
      wilt thou be pleas'd to come?
m   I with a perfect heart will walk
      within my house at home.

    3 I will endure no wicked thing
      before mine eyes to be:

7

PSALM CII.

Ver. 1-11. Dundee 144.   *Crowle* 153.
Ver. 12-22. St. Alphage 118.   *Belgrave* 110.
Ver. 23-28. St. Nicholas 151.   *St. Ann* 60.

p 1 O LORD, unto my pray'r give ear,
    my cry let come to thee;
2 And in the day of my distress
    hide not thy face from me.
Give ear to me; what time I call
    to answer me make haste:
3 For, as an hearth, my bones are burnt,
    my days, like smoke, do waste.

4 My heart within me smitten is,
    and it is withered
Like very grass; so that I do
    forget to eat my bread.
5 By reason of my groaning voice
    my bones cleave to my skin.
6 Like pelican in wilderness
    forsaken I have been:

I like an owl in desert am,
    that nightly there doth moan;

pp 7

p 9

pp 11

m 12

13 Thou shalt arise, and mercy have
    upon thy Sion yet;
  The time to favour her is come,   *m* 19
    the time that thou hast set.
14 For in her rubbish and her stones
    thy servants pleasure take;
  Yea, they the very dust thereof   20
    do favour for her sake.

15 So shall the heathen people fear
    the Lord's most holy name;
  And all the kings on earth shall dread *mf* 21
    thy glory and thy fame.
mf 16 When Sion by the mighty Lord
    built up again shall be,
  In glory then and majesty   22
    to men appear shall he.

mp 17 The prayer of the destitute
    he surely will regard;
  Their prayer will he not despise,   *p* 23
    by him it shall be heard.
mf 18 For generations yet to come
    this shall be on record: 24

mp My God, in mid-time of my days
    take thou me not away:
  From age to age eternally
    thy years endure and stay.

m 25 The firm foundation of the earth
    of old time thou hast laid;
  The heavens also are the work
    · which thine own hands have made.
26 Thou shalt for evermore endure,
mp   but they shall perish all;
  Yea, ev'ry one of them wax old,
    like to a garment, shall:

m   Thou, as a vesture, shalt them change,
    and they shall changed be:
27 But thou the same art, and thy years
    are to eternity.
28 The children of thy servants shall
    continually endure;
  And in thy sight, O Lord, their seed
    SHALL BE ESTABLISH'D SURE.

p

∧

V 3

4

PSALM CII.

pp 7 *And, sparrow-like, companionless,*
       Upon the house's top, I watch.

p 8 I all day long am made a scorn,
       Reproach'd by my malicious foes:
       The madmen are against me sworn,
       The men against me that arose.

p 9 For I have ashes eaten up,
       To me as if they had been bread;
       And with my drink I in my cup
       Of bitter tears a mixture made.

   10 Because thy wrath was not appeas'd,
       And dreadful indignation:
       Therefore it was that thou me rais'd,
       And thou again didst cast me down.

pp 11 *My days are like a shade alway,*
       Which doth declining swiftly pass;
       And I am withered away,
       Much like unto the fading grass.

m 12 But thou, O Lord, shalt still endure,
       From change and all mutation free,
       And to all generations sure
       Shall thy remembrance ever be.

13

14
p
m 15 All

mf 16

17

18

m 19

20
mf 21

/\ 22 When people and the kingdoms do
        Assemble all to praise the Lord.

p 23 My strength he weaken'd in the way
        My days of life he shortened.
mp 24 My God, O take me not away
        In mid-time of my days, I said:
m   Thy years throughout all ages last.
/\ 25 Of old thou hast established
        The earth's foundation firm and fast:
        Thy mighty hands the heav'ns have
        made.

mp 26 They perish shall, as garments do,
mf   But thou shalt evermore endure;
mp   As vestures, thou shalt change them so;
        And they shall all be changed sure:
f 27 BUT FROM ALL CHANGES THOU ART
        FREE;
        THY ENDLESS YEARS DO LAST FOR AYE.
     28 THY SERVANTS, AND THEIR SEED WHO
        BE,
        ESTABLISH'D SHALL BEFORE THEE STAY.

mf 1 O
        Be

2   O my s   God,
        forgetful be

mp 3

/\
mp 4
\/
mf

5

So that, ev'n as the eagle's age,
  renewed is thy youth.

6 God righteous judgment executes
  for all oppressed ones.

7 His ways to Moses, he his acts
  made known to Isr'el's sons.

mp 8 The Lord our God is merciful,
  and he is gracious,
Long-suffering, and slow to wrath,
  in mercy plenteous.

9 He will not chide continually,
  nor keep his anger still.

10 With us he dealt not as we sinn'd,
  nor did requite our ill.

m 11 For as the heaven in its height
  the earth surmounteth far;
So great to those that do him fear
  his tender mercies are:

12 As far as east is distant from
  the west, so far hath he
From us removed, in his love,
  all our iniquity.

mp 13

p 14

15

16

mf 17

∧

18

m 19

And ev'ry thing that being hath
his kingdom doth command.

mf 20 O ye his angels, that excel
in strength, bless ye the Lord;
Ye who obey what he commands,
and hearken to his word.

f 21 O BLESS AND MAGNIFY THE LORD,
YE GLORIOUS HOSTS OF HIS;
YE MINISTERS, THAT DO FULFIL
WHATE'ER HIS PLEASURE IS.

f

ff 22 O BLESS THE LORD, ALL YE HIS WORKS,
WHEREWITH THE WORLD IS STOR'D
IN HIS DOMINIONS EV'RY WHERE.
MY SOUL, BLESS THOU THE LORD.

m

:

PSALM CIV.

Dunfermline 47.   Old 68th 33.

mp

m 1 BLESS God, my soul. O Lord my
thou art exceeding great; [God,
With honour and with majesty
thou clothed art in state.

m

    Descend, unto that very place   15
      which thou for them didst found.
9 Thou hast a bound unto them set,
      that they may not pass over,
    That they do not return again   16
      the face of earth to cover.

10 He to the valleys sends the springs,
      which run among the hills:
11 They to all beasts of field give drink,   17
      wild asses drink their fills.
12 By them the fowls of heav'n shall have
      their habitation,
    Which do among the branches sing   18
      with delectation.

13 He from his chambers watereth
      the hills, when they are dry'd:
    With fruit and increase of thy works   19
      the earth is satisfy'd.
14 For cattle he makes grass to grow,
      he makes the herb to spring
    For th' use of man, that food to him   *utp* 20
      he from the earth may bring;

:

f 21 THE LIONS YOUNG ROAR FOR THEIR PREY,   *p* 29
m and seek their meat from God.

22 The sun doth rise, and home they flock,
 down in their dens they lie.

23 Man goes to work, his labour he   *m* 30
 doth to the ev'ning ply.

24 How manifold, Lord, are thy works!
 in wisdom wonderful
 Thou ev'ry one of them hast made;   *f* 31
 earth's of thy riches full:

25 So is this great and spacious sea,   *ff*
 wherein things creeping are,
 Which number'd cannot be; and beasts   *p* 32
 both great and small are there.

26 There ships go; there thou mak'st to
 that leviathan great. [play

27 These all wait on thee, that thou may'st   *f* 33
 in due time give them meat.

28 That which thou givest unto them
 they gather for their food;

mf Thine hand thou open'st lib'rally,   *m* 34
 they filled are with good.

⋀ And as for me, I will rejoice
   in God, my only Lord.
p 35 *From earth let sinners be consum'd,*
   let ill men no more be.
f   O THOU MY SOUL, BLESS THOU THE LORD.
   PRAISE TO THE LORD GIVE YE.

PSALM CV.

Ver. 1-7. *Dunfermline* 47.   St. *Alphage* 118.
Ver. 8.45. *Tallis* 93.   *Jackson's* 51.

mf 1 GIVE thanks to God, call on his name;
      to men his deeds make known.

  2 Sing ye to him, sing psalms; proclaim
     his wondrous works each one.

  3 See that ye in his holy name
     to glory do accord;
⋀ And let the heart of ev'ry one
   REJOICE THAT SEEKS THE LORD.

m 4 The Lord Almighty, and his strength,
    with stedfast hearts seek ye:
   His blessed and his gracious face
    seek ye continually.

5

10

A covenant to Israel,
  which ever should endure.
11 He said, I'll give Canaan's land   *mp* 18
    for heritage to you;
12 While they were strangers there, and   19
    in number very few: [few,
mp 13 While yet they went from land to land
    without a sure abode;
    And while through sundry kingdoms   *m* 20
    did wander far abroad;   [they
m 14 Yet, notwithstanding, suffer'd he
    no man to do them wrong:
    Yea, for their sakes, he did reprove   21
    kings, who were great and strong
15 Thus did he say, Touch ye not those
    that mine anointed be,
    Nor do the prophets any harm   22
    that do pertain to me.
mp 16 He call'd for famine on the land,
    he brake the staff of bread:
m 17 But yet he sent a man before,   23
    by whom they should be fed;

And Jacob also sojourned *mf* 32
 within the land of Ham.

24 And he did greatly by his pow'r   33
 increase his people there;
 And stronger than their enemies *m* 34
 they by his blessing were.

25 Their heart he turned to envy   35
 his folk maliciously,
 With those that his own servants were *mp* 36
 to deal in subtilty.

26 His servant Moses he did send, *f* 37
 Aaron his chosen one.

27 By these his signs and wonders great
 in Ham's land were made known. *m* 38
p 28 *Darkness he sent, and made it dark;*
m   his word they did obey.   39

29 He turn'd their waters into blood,
 and he their fish did slay.   40

30 The land in plenty brought forth frogs
 in chambers of their kings.

31 His word all sorts of flies and lice ∧ 41
 in all their borders brings.

42 For on his holy promise he,
    and servant Abr'ham, thought.

f 43 WITH JOY HIS PEOPLE, HIS ELECT
    WITH GLADNESS, FORTH HE BROUGHT.

m 44 And unto them the pleasant lands
    he of the heathen gave;
    That of the people's labour they
    inheritance might have.

45 That they his statutes might observe
    according to his word;
    And that they might his laws obey.
f   GIVE PRAISE UNTO THE LORD.

PSALM CVI.

Ver. 1-5 *Dunfermline* 47.   *St. David* 48.
Ver. 6-45. *Old* 137th 35.   *Farrant* 58.

mf 1 GIVE praise and thanks unto the
    for bountiful is he;   [Lord,
    His tender mercy doth endure
    unto eternity.

2 God's mighty works who can express?
    or shew forth all his praise?

3

mp 4

m 5

p 6

m 7

Wi

di

s.

;

:

mf 8 Nevertheless he saved them,
  ev'n for his own name's sake;
  That so he might to be well known
   his mighty power make.

 m 9 When he the Red sea did rebuke,
  then dried up it was:
  Through depths, as through the wilder-
  he safely made them pass. [ness,
  10 From hands of those that hated them
   he did his people save;
  And from the en'my's cruel hand
   to them redemption gave.

mf 11 The waters overwhelm'd their foes;
  not one was left alive.
  12 Then they believ'd his word, and praise
   to him in songs did give.
mp 13 But soon did they his mighty works
  forget unthankfully,
  And on his counsel and his will
   did not wait patiently;

  14 But much did lust in wilderness,
  and God in desert tempt.

15

16

17

18

19

20

21 They did forget the mighty God,   *p*
    that had their saviour been,
  By whom such great things brought to   *m* 29
    they had in Egypt seen.   [pass
mf 22 In Ham's land he did wondrous works,
    things terrible did he,
  When he his mighty hand and arm   30
    stretch'd out at the Red sea.

mp 23 Then said he, He would them destroy,   31
    had not, his wrath to stay,
  His chosen Moses stood in breach,   32
    that them he should not slay.
m 24 Yea, they despis'd the pleasant land,
    believed not his word :
25 But in their tents they murmured,   33
    not heark'ning to the Lord.

26 Therefore in desert them to slay
    he lifted up his hand :
27 'Mong nations to o'erthrow their seed,   34
    and scatter in each land.
28 They unto Baal-poor did   35
    themselves associate;

36 And they their idols serv'd, which did
    a snare unto them turn.
p 37 *Their sons and daughters they to dev'ls*
    in sacrifice did burn.

38 *In their own children's guiltless blood*
    their hands they did imbrue,
    Whom to Canaan's idols they
    for sacrifices slew:
    So was the land defil'd with blood.
mp 39   They stain'd with their own way,
    And with their own inventions   *mf* 47
    a whoring they did stray.

40 Against his people kindled was
    the wrath of God therefore,
    Insomuch that he did his own   *f* 48
    inheritance abhor.
41 He gave them to the heathen's hand;
    their foes did them command.
42 Their en'mies them oppress'd, they were
    made subject to their hand.

m 43 He many times deliver'd them;   *mf*
p   *But with their counsel so*

2 Let God's redeem'd say so, whom he
   from th' en'my's hand did free;
3 And gather'd them out of the lands,
   from north, south, east, and west.
mp 4 They stray'd in desert's pathless way,
   no city found to rest.

5 For thirst and hunger in them faints
6   their soul. When straits them press,
   They cry unto the Lord, and he
   them frees from their distress.
m 7 Them also in a way to walk
   that right is he did guide,
   That they might to a city go,
   wherein they might abide.

mf 8 O that men to the Lord would give
   praise for his goodness then,
   And for his works of wonder done
   unto the sons of men!
9 For he the soul that longing is
   doth fully satisfy;
   With goodness he the hungry soul
   doth fill abundantly.

mp 10

11

p 12

13
m 14

mf 15

ff 16

       By him in sunder also cut   ∧ 25
         THE BARS OF IRON WERE.

mp 17 Fools, for their sin, and their offence,
       do sore affliction bear;

∨ 18 All kind of meat their soul abhors;   ∨ 26
     they to death's gates draw near.

m 19 *In grief they cry to God;* he saves
      them from their miseries.

∧ 20 He sends his word, them heals, and them   *m* 27
     from their destructions frees.

mf 21 O that men to the Lord would give   ∧ 28
     praise for his goodness then,
     And for his works of wonder done   > 29
     unto the sons of men!

f 22 AND LET THEM SACRIFICE TO HIM   <
     OFF'RINGS OF THANKFULNESS;   *p*
     AND LET THEM SHEW ABROAD HIS WORKS *m* 30
     IN SONGS OF JOYFULNESS.

m 23 Who go to sea in ships, and in
     great waters trading be,

   24 Within the deep these men God's works *mf* 31
     and his great wonders see.

<   And for his works of wonder done | *p* 39
       unto the sons of men!
f 32 AMONG THE PEOPLE GATHERED
      LET THEM EXALT HIS NAME;
      AMONG ASSEMBLED ELDERS SPREAD   *mp* 40
      HIS MOST RENOWNED FAME.

mp 33 He to dry land turns water-springs,
      and floods to wilderness;
  34 For sins of those that dwell therein,   *m* 41
      fat land to barrenness.
m 35 The burnt and parched wilderness
      to water-pools he brings;
     The ground that was dry'd up before   *mf* 42
      he turns to water-springs:

  36 And there, for dwelling, he a place
      doth to the hungry give,
     That they a city may prepare
      commodiously to live.   43
  37 There sow they fields, and vineyards
      to yield fruits of increase.   [plant,
  38 His blessing makes them multiply,
      lets not their beasts decrease.

PSALM CVIII.

Ver. 1-6 St. George 52.   *York 46.*
Ver. 7-13 Glasgow 77.   *St. Magnus 45*

8

m 1 MY heart is fix'd, Lord; I will sing
    and with my glory praise.
mf 2 Awake up psaltery and harp;
    myself I'll early raise.
    3 I'll praise thee 'mong the people, Lord;
    'mong nations sing will I:
    4 For above heav'n thy mercy's great,
    thy truth doth reach the sky.

10

    5 Be thou above the heavens, Lord,
    exalted gloriously;
    Thy glory all the earth above
    be lifted up on high.
mp 6 That those who thy beloved are
    delivered may be,
    O do thou save with thy right hand,
    and answer give to me.

p 11

m 12

f 13

m 7 God in his holiness hath said,
    Herein I will take pleasure;

PSALM CIX.

Martyrs 148.   *St. Nicholas* 151.

m 1 O THOU the God of all my praise,
     do thou not hold thy peace;
mp 2 For mouths of wicked men to speak
     against me do not cease:
     The mouths of vile deceitful men
     against me open'd be;
     And with a false and lying tongue
     they have accused me.

   3 They did beset me round about
     with words of hateful spight:
     And though to them no cause I gave,
     against me they did fight.
   4 They for my love became my foes,
     but I me set to pray.
   5 Evil for good, hatred for love,
     to me they did repay.

   6 Set thou the wicked over him;
     and upon his right hand
     Give thou his greatest enemy,
     ev'n Satan, leave to stand.

10

11

12

13

And in the foll'wing age their name
  be blotted out by thee.
14 Let God his father's wickedness
  still to remembrance call;
And never let his mother's sin
  be blotted out at all.

15 But let them all before the Lord
  appear continually,
That he may wholly from the earth
  cut off their memory.
16 Because he mercy minded not
  but persecuted still
The poor and needy, that he might
  the broken-hearted kill.

17 As he in cursing pleasure took
  so let it to him fall;
As he delighted not to bless
  so bless him not at all.
18 As cursing he like clothes put on
  into his bowels. so,
Like water, and into his bones,
  like oil, down let it go.

19

20

m 21

p 22

pp 23

24

mp 25

And they that did upon me look
did shake their heads at me.

m 26 O do thou help and succour me,
who art my God and Lord:
And, for thy tender mercy's sake,
safety to me afford:

27 That thereby they may know that this
is thy almighty hand;
And that thou, Lord, hast done the same,
they may well understand.

mp 28 Although they curse with spite, yet,
bless thou with loving voice: [Lord,
Let them asham'd be when they rise;
thy servant let rejoice.

29 Let thou mine adversaries all
with shame be clothed over;
And let their own confusion
them, as a mantle, cover.

mf 30 But as for me, I with my mouth
will greatly praise the Lord;
AND I AMONG THE MULTITUDE
HIS PRAISES WILL RECORD.

f 5 THE GLORIOUS AND MIGHTY LORD,
 THAT SITS AT THY RIGHT HAND,
 SHALL, IN HIS DAY OF WRATH, STRIKE
  THROUGH
 KINGS THAT DO HIM WITHSTAND.
 6 HE SHALL AMONG THE HEATHEN JUDGE,

mp he shall with bodies dead
 The places fill: o'er many lands
 he wound shall ev'ry head.

m 7 The brook that runneth in the way
 with drink shall him supply;
 And, for this cause, in triumph he
 shall lift his head on high.

3

m 4

mp

m

PSALM CXI.

Colchester 111L *Dunfermline* 47. *Old Winchester* 128

mf 1 PRAISE ye the Lord: with my whole
 I will God's praise declare, [heart
 Where the assemblies of the just
 and congregations are.

m 2 The whole works of the Lord our God
 are great above all measure,

mf

9 He sent redemption to his folk·
    his covenant for aye
p He did command: *holy his name*
    and rev'rend is alway.

m 10 Wisdom's beginning is God's fear:
    good understanding they
    Have all that his commands fulfil:
    his praise endures for aye.

PSALM CXII.

Arnold's 66.   Chichester 122.   Canterbury 140.

f 1 PRAISE YE THE LORD. The man is
m   bless'd
    that fears the Lord aright,
    He who in his commandements
    doth greatly take delight.
2 His seed and offspring powerful
    shall be the earth upon:
    Of upright men blessed shall be
    the generation.

3 Riches and wealth shall ever be
    within his house in store;

4

mp
m

5

mf

mp
mf

m 9 He hath dispers'd, giv'n to the poor;
    his righteousness shall be
Λ   To ages all; with honour shall
    his horn be raised high.
mp 10 The wicked shall it see, and fret,
    his teeth gnash, melt away:
m   What wicked men do most desire
V   shall utterly decay.

PSALM CXIII.

Chingford 91.   *Old Glasgow* 121.

mf 1 PRAISE God: ye servants of the
    Lord,
    O praise, the Lord's name praise.
2 Yea, blessed be the name of God
    from this time forth always.
3 From rising sun to where it sets,
    God's name is to be prais'd.
4 Above all nations God is high,
    'bove heav'ns his glory rais'd.

5 Unto the Lord our God that dwells
    on high, who can compare?

Λ 8

Λ
Λ
f

m

mf 2

: '

p 3 *The sea it saw, and quickly fled,*
∧   Jordan was driven back.

m 4 Like rams the mountains, and like lambs
       the hills skipp'd to and fro.

5 O sea, why fledd'st thou? Jordan, back
   why wast thou driven so?

6 Ye mountains great, wherefore was it
   that ye did skip like rams?
   And wherefore was it, little hills,
   that ye did leap like lambs?

mp 7 O at the presence of the Lord,
∨   *earth, tremble thou for fear,*
m   While as the presence of the God
       of Jacob doth appear:

8 Who from the hard and stony rock
   did standing water bring;
   And by his pow'r did turn the flint
   into a water-spring.

PSALM CXV.

Ver. 1-11 *Tallis* 93.   *St. Simon* 43.
Ver. 12-18 *St. Mirren* 97.   *New St. Ann* 117.

m 1 NOT unto us, Lord, not to us,
       but do thou glory take
   Unto thy name, ev'n for thy truth,
   and for thy mercy's sake.

mp 2 O wherefore should the heathen say,
       Where is their God now gone?

mf 3 But our God in the heavens is,
       what pleas'd him he hath done.

m 4 Their idols silver are and gold,
       work of men's hands they be.

5 Mouths have they, but they do not speak;
   and eyes, but do not see;

6 Ears have they, but they do not hear;
   noses, but savour not;

7 Hands, feet, but handle not, nor walk;
   nor speak they through their throat.

8 Like them their makers are, and all
   on them their trust that build.

f 9 O ISR'EL, TRUST THOU IN THE LORD,
∧   HE IS THEIR HELP AND SHIELD.

mf 10 O Aaron's house, trust in the Lord,
∧   THEIR HELP AND SHIELD IS HE.

mf 11 Ye that fear God, trust in the Lord,
    THEIR HELP AND SHIELD HE'LL BE.

mf 12 The Lord of us hath mindful been,
    and he will bless us still:
    He will the house of Isr'el bless,   *pp*
    bless Aaron's house he will.

13 Both small and great, that fear the   *m*   4
    he will them surely bless.   [Lord,
14 The Lord will you, you and your seed,   *mp*
    AYE MORE AND MORE INCREASE.

mf 15 O blessed are ye of the Lord,   *m*
    who made the earth and heav'n.

16 The heav'n, ev'n heav'ns, are God's, but
    earth to men's sons hath giv'n.   [he

p 17 *The dead, nor who to silence go,*
    God's praise do not record.

f 18 BUT HENCEFORTH WE FOR EVER WILL   thy
    BLESS GOD. PRAISE YE THE LORD.   gely

PSALM CXVI.
Ferrey 136.   *Manchester 70.*

m 1 I LOVE the Lord, because my voice
    and prayers he did hear.

9 I in the land of those that live
    will walk the Lord before.
10 I did believe, therefore I spake:
mp   I was afflicted sore.
11 I said, when I was in my haste,
    that all men liars be.
12 What shall I render to the Lord
    for all his gifts. to me?
mf 13 I'll of salvation take the cup,
    on God's name will I call:
14 I'll pay my vows now to the Lord
    before his people all.
mp 15 Dear in God's sight is his saints' death.
16   Thy servant, Lord, am I ;
    Thy servant sure, thine handmaid's son:
    my bands thou didst untie.
mf 17 Thank-off'rings I to thee will give,
    and on God's name will call.
18 I'll pay my vows now to the Lord
    before his people all;
19 Within the courts of God's own house,
    within the midst of thee,.

O city of Jerusalem.
f   PRAISE TO THE LORD GIVE YE.

mf

:

p	5	*I in distress call'd on the Lord;*	
m		the Lord did answer me:	
∧		He in a large place did me set,	*m* 12
		from trouble made me free.	
mf	6	The mighty Lord is on my side,	∧
		I will not be afraid;	
∧		For anything that man can do	*mp* 13
		I SHALL NOT BE DISMAY'D.	*m*
mf	7	The Lord doth take my part with them	∧ 14
		that help to succour me:	
		Therefore on those that do me hate	*m* 15
		I my desire shall see.	
m	8	Better it is to trust in God	∧
		than trust in man's defence;	
∧	9	Better to trust in God than make	*mf* 16
		princes our confidence.	
m	10	The nations, joining all in one,	
		did compass me about:	
∧		But in the Lord's most holy name	*m* 17
		I shall them all root out.	
m	11	They compass'd me about; I say,	*p* 18
		they compass'd me about:	∧

mf 19   O set ye open unto me
        the gates of righteousness;
    Then will I enter into them,
        AND I THE LORD WILL BLESS.

mf 20   This is the gate of God, by it
        the just shall enter in.
  21 THEE WILL I PRAISE, FOR THOU ME
        HEARD'ST,
    AND HAST MY SAFETY BEEN.
mf 22   That stone is made head corner-stone,
        which builders did despise:
  23 THIS IS THE DOING OF THE LORD,
    AND WONDROUS IN OUR EYES.

f 24 THIS IS THE DAY GOD MADE, IN IT
    WE'LL JOY TRIUMPHANTLY.
m 25 Save now, I pray thee, Lord; I pray,
    send now prosperity.
mf 26 Blessed is he in God's great name
        that cometh us to save:
    We, from the house which to the Lord
        pertains, you blessed have.

4 Thou hast commanded us to keep
   thy precepts carefully.
5 O that thy statutes to observe   11
   thou would'st my ways direct!

⋀ 6 Then shall I not be sham'd, when I   12
   thy precepts all respect.

m 7 Then with integrity of heart   13
   thee will I praise and bless,
   When I the judgments all have learn'd ⋀ 14
   of thy pure righteousness.

⋀ 8 That I will keep thy statutes all   m 15
   firmly resolv'd have I:
mp O do not then, most gracious God,
   forsake me utterly.

       BETH. *The Second Part.*   16
Bishopthorpe 109.   *New St. Ann* 117.   *Canterbury* 140.
m 9 By what means shall a young man learn ⋀
   his way to purify?
   If he according to thy word
   thereto attentive be.
10 Unfeignedly thee have I sought   mp 17
   with all my soul and heart:

That by thy favour I may live
  and duly keep thy word.
18 Open mine eyes, that of thy law
  the wonders I may see.
19 I am a stranger on this earth,
  hide not thy laws from me.

p 20 *My soul within me breaks, and doth*
   much fainting still endure,
m   Through longing that it hath all times
  unto thy judgments pure.
21 Thou hast rebuk'd the cursed proud,
  who from thy precepts swerve.
mp 22 Reproach and shame remove from me,
  for I thy laws observe.

23 Against me princes spake with spite,
  while they in council sat:
  But I thy servant did upon
  thy statutes meditate.
m 24 My comfort, and my heart's delight,
  thy testimonies be;
  And they, in all my doubts and fears,
  are counsellors to me.

mp 25
26
27

p 28

29

m 30

31 I to thy testimonies cleave ;
    shame do not on me cast.
32 I'll run thy precepts' way, when thou
    my heart enlarged hast.

HE. *The Fifth Part.*
Farrant 58.   *Howard* 115.

mp 33 Teach me, O Lord, the perfect way
    of thy precepts divine,
    And to observe it to the end
    I shall my heart incline.
m 34 Give understanding unto me
    so keep thy law shall I
    Yea, ev'n with my whole heart I shall
    observe it carefully.
m 35 In thy law's path make me to go;
    for I delight therein.
36 My heart unto thy testimonies
    and not to greed, incline.
37 Turn thou away my sight and eyes
    from viewing vanity ;
    And in thy good and holy way
    be pleas'd to quicken me.

38

mp 39

40   in

mp 41

   ac

m 42

43

    thy
my hope

44 So shall I keep for evermore
    thy law continually.

45 And, sith that I thy precepts seek,
    I'll walk at liberty.

mf 46 I'll speak thy word to kings, and I
    with shame shall not be mov'd;

47 And will delight myself always
    in thy laws, which I lov'd.

m 48 To thy commandments, which I lov'd,
    my hands lift up I will;

And I will also meditate
    upon thy statutes still.

ZAIN. *The Seventh Part.*
St. James 98.   *St. Andrew* 72.

mp 49 Remember, Lord, thy gracious word
    thou to thy servant spake,

Which, for a ground of my sure hope,
    thou causedst me to take.

m 50 This word of thine my comfort is
    in mine affliction:

For in my straits I am reviv'd
    by this thy word alone.

mp 51

m

52

p 53

m 54

55

56

m 57

mf

York 46.

m 58 With my whole heart I did entreat
    thy face and favour free:
    According to thy gracious word
    be merciful to me.

59 I thought upon my former ways,
    and did my life well try;
    And to thy testimonies pure
    my feet then turned I.

60 I did not stay, nor linger long,
    as those that slothful are;
    But hastily thy laws to keep
    myself I did prepare.

61 Bands of ill men me robb'd; yet I
    thy precepts did not slight.

62 I'll rise at midnight thee to praise,
    ev'n for thy judgments right.

63 I am companion to all those
    who fear, and thee obey.

64 O Lord, thy mercy fills the earth:
    teach me thy laws, I pray.

            TETH. *The Ninth Part.*
            Farrant 58.   *Comfort* 127.

mp 60

∧

∧

⋀ Than many thousands and great sums
   of gold and silver be.

       JOD.   *The Tenth Part.*
       Evan 125.   *St. James 98.*

mp 73 Thou mad'st and fashion'dst me: thy
   to know give wisdom, Lord. [laws
⋀ 74 So who thee fear shall joy to see
   me trusting in thy word.
m 75 That very right thy judgments are
   I know, and do confess;
   And that thou hast afflicted me
   in truth and faithfulness.
mp 76 O let thy kindness merciful,
   I pray thee, comfort me,
   As to thy servant faithfully
   was promised by thee.
   77 And let thy tender mercies come
   to me, that I may live;
   Because thy holy laws to me
   sweet delectation give.
   78 Lord, let the proud ashamed be;
   for they, without a cause,

79

80

p 81

82

pp
83

m

p 84

85

:

86 Thy words all faithful are: help me,
 pursu'd without a cause.

pp 87 *They so consum'd me, that on earth*
 my life they scarce did leave ·

m Thy precepts yet forsook I not,
 but close to them did cleave.

88 After thy loving-kindness, Lord
 me quicken, and preserve:
 The testimony of thy mouth
 so shall I still observe.

  LAMED. *The Twelfth Part.*
 Palestrina 92. Peckham 71. Durham 95.

m 89 Thy word for ever is, O Lord,
 in heaven settled fast;

90 Unto all generations
 thy faithfulness doth last:
 The earth thou hast established,
 and it abides by thee.

91 This day they stand as thou ordain'dst;
 for all thy servants be.

92 Unless in thy most perfect law
 my soul delights had found,

93

94

*mp*95

m 96

m 97

98

99

PSALM CXIX.

Because my meditation
    thy testimonies are.

100 In understanding I excel
    those that are ancients;
    For I endeavoured to keep
    all thy commandements.

101 My feet from each ill **way** I stay'd,
    that I may keep thy word.
102 I from thy judgments have not swerv'd;
    for thou hast taught me, Lord.

mp 103 How sweet unto my taste, O Lord,
    are all thy words of truth!

Yea, I do find them sweeter far
    than honey to my mouth.

m 104 I through thy precepts, that are pure,
    do understanding get;
    I therefore every way that's false
    with all my heart do hate.

NUN. *The Fourteenth Part.*
Solomon 103.   Jackson's 51.

m 105 Thy word is to my feet a lamp
    and to my path a light.

mf 106

p 107

m

108

p 109
m
110

111

    for they my
mp 112   fully

SAMECH. *The Fifteenth Part.*
Abbey 56. *Harrington 120.*

p 120

m 113 I hate the thoughts of vanity,
but love thy law do I.

mf 114 My shield and hiding-place thou art:
I on thy word rely.

m 115 All ye that evil-doers are
from me depart away;

mf For the commandments of my God
I purpose to obey.

m 121

mp 116 According to thy faithful word
uphold and stablish me,

⋀ That I may live, and of my hope
ashamed never be.

122

mp 117 Hold thou me up, so shall I be
in peace and safety still;

⋀ And to thy statutes have respect
continually I will.

mp 123

m 118 Thou tread'st down all that love to
false their deceit doth prove [stray;

124

119 Lewd men, like dross, away thou
therefore thy law I love. [putt'st;

125

:

mf 126 'Tis time thou work, Lord; for they
    made void thy law divine.   [have
  127 Therefore thy precepts more I love
    than gold, yea, gold most fine.
  128 Concerning all things thy commands
    all right I judge therefore;
    AND EV'RY FALSE AND WICKED WAY
    I PERFECTLY ABHOR.

PE.   *The Seventeenth Part.*
Morven 99.   *St. Mary* 145.   *Farrant* 58.

mp 129 Thy statutes, Lord, are wonderful,
    my soul them keeps with care.
  130 The entrance of thy words gives light,
    makes wise who simple are.
  131 My mouth I have wide opened,
    and panted earnestly,
    While after thy commandements
    I long'd exceedingly.

p 132 *Look on me, Lord, and merciful*
    do thou unto me prove,
    As thou art wont to do to those
    thy name who truly love.

m 133

134

135

p 136

138

139

:

forgotten have,
aws despise.

140 Thy word's most pure, therefore on it
    thy servant's love is set.

p 141 *Small, and despis'd I am, yet I*
    thy precepts not forget.

f 142 THY RIGHTEOUSNESS IS RIGHTEOUS-
    WHICH EVER DOTH ENDURE: [NESS
    THY HOLY LAW, LORD, ALSO IS
    THE VERY TRUTH MOST PURE.

p 143 *Trouble and anguish have me found,*
    and taken hold on me:

m   Yet in my trouble my delight
    thy just commandments be.

f 144 ETERNAL RIGHTEOUSNESS IS IN
    THY TESTIMONIES ALL:

m   Lord, to me understanding give,
⋀   and ever live I shall.

      KOPH. *The Nineteenth Part.*
      Dundee 144.   *Walsal 155.*

mp 145 With my whole heart I cry'd, Lord,
    I will thy word obey.   [hear;

⋀ 146 I cry'd to thee; save me, and I
    will keep thy laws alway.

p 147

⋀

mp 148   sly
                       nig

149   :

⋀   thy ju
        revive and quicke

mp 150

⋀ 151   all

mf 152

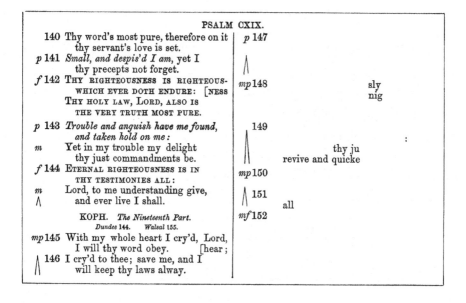

PSALM CXIX.

mp 153 Consider mine affliction,
 in safety do me set :
Deliver me, O Lord, for I
 thy law do not forget.
154 After thy word revive thou me ;
 save me, and plead my cause.
155 Salvation is from sinners far ;
 for they seek not thy laws.

m 156 O Lord, both great and manifold
 thy tender mercies be .
⋀ According to thy judgments just,
 revive and quicken me.
mp 157 My persecutors many are,
 and foes that do combine ;
⋀ Yet from thy testimonies pure
 my heart doth not decline.
p 158 *I saw transgressors, and was griev'd ;*
 for they keep not thy word.
m 159 See how I love thy law ! as thou
 art kind, me quicken, Lord.
⋀ 160 From the beginning all thy word
 hath been most true and sure :

⋀ Thy righteous judgments ev'ry one
 FOR EVERMORE ENDURE.

mp 161

m 162

163

164

165

166

167

On them my heart is set, and them
I love exceedingly.
168 Thy testimonies and thy laws
I kept with special care;
For all my works and ways each one
before thee open are.

TAU. *The Twenty-second Part.*
Old Carlisle 129.   Farrant 58.
mp 169 O let my earnest pray'r and cry
come near before thee, Lord:
Give understanding unto me
according to thy word.
170 Let my request before thee come:
after thy word me free.
m 171 My lips shall utter praise, when thou

174

175

p 176
m

p 1
m

salvation, Lord,

:

2. Fr   wing   an   ongue

That I in tabernacles dwell
 to Kedar that belong.
6 My soul with him that hateth peace
 hath long a dweller been.
7 I am for peace; but when I speak,
 for battle they are keen.

◊ 8

m 1

PSALM CXXI.
French 44. *Tallis 93.*

m 1 I TO the hills will lift mine eyes,
 from whence doth come mine aid.
f 2 MY SAFETY COMETH FROM THE LORD,
 WHO HEAV'N AND EARTH HATH MADE.
m 3 Thy foot he'll not let slide, nor will
 he slumber that thee keeps.
◊ 4 Behold, he that keeps Israel,
 he slumbers not, nor sleeps.
m 5 The Lord thee keeps, the Lord thy
 on thy right hand doth stay: [shade
mf 6 The moon by night thee shall not
 nor yet the sun by day. [smite,
7 The Lord shall keep thy soul; he shall
 preserve thee from all ill.

3

:

 ,
:

mp 6

m

mf

:

AND EVER MAY THY PALACES
PROSPERITY RETAIN.

m 8 Now, for my friends' and brethren's
Peace be in thee, I'll say.   [sakes,
9 And for the house of God our Lord,
I'll seek thy good alway.

PSALM CXXIII.
Denfield 124.   *Evan* 125.

mp 1 O THOU that dwellest in the heav'ns,
I lift mine eyes to thee.

2 Behold, as servants' eyes do look
their masters' hand to see,
As handmaid's eyes her mistress' hand;
so do our eyes attend
Upon the Lord our God, until
to us he mercy send.

p 3 O Lord, be gracious to us,
unto us gracious be;
Because replenish'd with contempt
exceedingly are we.

mp 4 Our soul is fill'd with scorn of those
that at their ease abide,

m 1 H may

2

3

p 4

m 5

f 6

mf 7

f 8

[TEETH

N

HIS NAME WHO DID THE HEAV'N CREATE, | *p*
AND WHO THE EARTH DID FRAME.

Another of the same.
Old 124th 176.

m 1 NOW Israel   *p*
      may say, and that truly,
    If that the Lord   *f* 6
      had not our cause maintain'd;
    2 If that the Lord
      had not our right sustain'd,
    When cruel men
      against us furiously
    Rose up in wrath,   *mf* 7
      to make of us their prey;
    3 Then certainly
      they had devour'd us all
    And swallow'd quick,
      for ought that we could deem;
    Such was their rage,   *ff* 8
      as we might well esteem.
    4 And as fierce floods
      before them all things drown,

PSALM CXXV.

St. David 48.   *Grafenberg* 139.

mf 1 THEY in the Lord that firmly trust
shall be like Sion hill,
Which at no time can be remov'd,
but standeth ever still.

m 2 As round about Jerusalem
the mountains stand alway,
The Lord his folk doth compass so,
from henceforth and for aye.

mp 3 For ill men's rod upon the lot
of just men shall not lie;
Lest righteous men stretch forth their
unto iniquity.   [hands
4 Do thou to all those that be good
thy goodness, Lord, impart;
And do thou good to those that are
upright within their heart.

p 5 *But as for such as turn aside*
after their crooked way,
God shall lead forth with wicked men:
mf   on Isr'el peace shall stay.

PSALM CXXVI.

Abbey 56   *York* 46

mf 2

m

mf 3

mp 4

mf 5

m 6

p
f

SHEAVES,
REJOICING SHALL RETURN.

PSALM CXXVII.
St. Ann 60.   *French* 44.

m 1 EXCEPT the Lord do build the house,
　　　　the builders lose their pain:
　　Except the Lord the city keep,
　　　　the watchmen watch in vain.

　 2 'Tis vain for you to rise betimes,
　　　　or late from rest to keep,
　　To feed on sorrow's bread; so gives
　　　　he his beloved sleep.

m 3 Lo, children are God's heritage,
　　　　the womb's fruit his reward.

　 4 The sons of youth as arrows are,
　　　　for strong men's hands prepar'd.

　 5 O happy is the man that hath
　　　　his quiver fill'd with those ·

mf 　They unashamed in the gate
　　　　shall speak unto their foes.

PSALM CXXVIII.
Philippi 116.　　　*Belgrave* 110.

m 1 BLESS'D is each one that fears the
　　　and walketh in his ways;　[Lord,

ʌ 2

m 3 Thy wife
　　　　by thy
　　　　　chil
　　about thy table round.

mf 4

m 5

　　 6

m 1

　　 2

mp 3

mf 4 The righteous Lord did cut the cords
    of the ungodly crew.

m 5 Let Sion's haters all be turn'd
    back with confusion.

  6 As grass on houses' tops be they,
    which fades ere it be grown:

  7 Whereof enough to fill his hand
    the mower cannot find;
    Nor can the man his bosom fill,
    whose work is sheaves to bind.

  8 Neither say they who do go by,
    God's blessing on you rest:
    We in the name of God the Lord
    do wish you to be blest.

PSALM CXXX.
Martyrdom 64.

p 1 *LORD, from the depths to thee I cry'd.*
  2 *My voice, Lord, do thou hear:*
    Unto my supplication's voice
    give an attentive ear.

pp 3 *Lord, who shall stand, if thou, O Lord,*
    should'st mark iniquity?

7

8   is ever found with him.

mp 2 I surely have
    with quiet   mild,

As child of mother wean'd: my soul
is like a weaned child.

mf 3 Upon the Lord let all the hope
of Israel rely,
Ev'n from the time that present is
unto eternity.

PSALM CXXXII.

Ver. 1-10 Brunswick 101.   Dalkeith 85.
Ver. 11-18 York Minster 134.   St. Mirren 97.

mp 1 DAVID, and his afflictions all,
Lord, do thou think upon;

m 2 How unto God he sware, and vow'd
to Jacob's mighty One.

3 I will not come within my house,
nor rest in bed at all;

4 Nor shall mine eyes take any sleep
nor eyelids slumber shall;

5 Till for the Lord a place I find
where he may make abode·
A place of habitation
for Jacob's mighty God.

6 Lo, at the place of Ephratah
of it we understood;
And we did find it in the fields,
and city of the wood.

7 We'll go into his tabernacles
p   *and at his footstool bow.*
mf 8 Arise, O Lord, into thy rest,
th' ark of thy strength, and thou.

9 O let thy priests be clothed, Lord,
with truth and righteousness;
And let all those that are thy saints
SHOUT LOUD FOR JOYFULNESS.

m 10 For thine own servant David's sake,
do not deny thy grace;
Nor of thine own anointed one
turn thou away the face.

11 The Lord in truth to David sware,
he will not turn from it,
I of thy body's fruit will make
upon thy throne to sit.

12 My cov'nant if thy sons will keep,
and laws to them made known,

Their children then shall also sit
    for ever on thy throne.   in
13 For God of Sion hath made choice;
    there he desires to dwell.
mp 14 This is my rest, here still I'll stay;
    for I do like it well.

15 Her food I'll greatly bless; her poor
    with bread will satisfy.   [saints
16 Her priests I'll clothe with health; her
    SHALL SHOUT FORTH JOYFULLY.
m 17 And there will I make David's horn
    to bud forth pleasantly:
    For him that mine anointed is
    a lamp ordain'd have I.

18 As with a garment I will clothe   *mf*
    with shame his en'mies all:
    But yet the crown that he doth wear
    upon him flourish shall.

PSALM CXXXIII.
Moravia 87.   *Northampton* 119.

m 1 BEHOLD, how good a thing it is,
    and how becoming well,

PSALM CXXXV.

St. Stephen 62.   *Old Winchester* 128.

mf 1 PRAISE ye the Lord, the Lord's
   name praise;
 his servants, praise ye God.

 2 Who stand in God's house, in the
  of our God make abode. [courts
 3 Praise ye the Lord, for he is good;
  unto him praises sing:
 Sing praises to his name, because
  it is a pleasant thing.

 4 For Jacob to himself the Lord
  did choose of his good pleasure
 And he hath chosen Israel
  for his peculiar treasure.

f 5 BECAUSE I KNOW ASSUREDLY
  THE LORD IS VERY GREAT,
 AND THAT OUR LORD ABOVE ALL GODS
  IN GLORY HATH HIS SEAT.

mf 6 What things soever pleas'd the Lord,
  that in the heav'n did he,

    7

p 8
  9

m 10
  11

  12

mf 13

14 *For why?* the righteous God will judge
    his people righteously;
    Concerning those that do him serve,
    himself repent will he.

m 15 The idols of the nations
    of silver are and gold,
    And by the hands of men is made
    their fashion and mould.

16 Mouths have they, but they do not
    eyes, but they do not see; [speak;
17 Ears have they, but hear not; and in
    their mouths no breathing be.
18 Their makers are like them; so are
    all that on them rely.

f 19 O ISR'EL'S HOUSE, BLESS GOD; BLESS
    O AARON'S FAMILY.   [GOD,

mf 20 O bless the Lord, of Levi's house
    ye who his servants are;
    And bless the holy name of God,
    all ye the Lord that fear.

f 21 AND BLESSED BE THE LORD OUR GOD
    FROM SION'S HOLY HILL,

Greyfriars 178.

mf 1		:
2		:
3		:
4	:	
5		:
6	for	
7		:
8	:	
9		:

p 10 *Who Egypt's first-born kill'd outright:*   21   :
mf   for his grace faileth never.
   11 And Isr'el brought from Egypt land: 22   :
       for mercy hath he ever.
   12 With stretch'd-out arm, and with strong *mp* 23   :
       for his grace faileth never. [hand: *mf*
   13 By whom the Red sea parted was: 24
       for mercy hath he ever.
   14 And through its midst made Isr'el   *m* 25   :
       for his grace faileth never. [pass:
   15 But Phar'oh and his host did drown: *ff* 26   :
       for mercy hath he ever.
   16 Who through the desert led his own:
       for his grace faileth never.

   17 To him great kings who overthrew: *mf* 1   :
       for he hath mercy ever.
   18 Yea, famous kings in battle slew: 2
       for his grace faileth never.   :
   19 Ev'n Sihon king of Amorites:
       for he hath mercy ever.
   20 And Og the king of Bashanites:
       for his grace faileth never.

mf 3 The Lord of lords praise ye,
    Whose mercies still endure.
   4 Great wonders only he
    Doth work by his great pow'r:
       For certainly, &c.

   5 Which God omnipotent,   *mp* 10
    By might and wisdom high,
    The heav'n and firmament
    Did frame, as we may see:
       For certainly, &c.   *mf*

   6 To him who did outstretch   11
    This earth so great and wide,
    Above the waters' reach   12 With a
    Making it to abide:
       For certainly, &c.

   7 Great lights he made to be;   13
    For his grace lasteth aye:
   8 Such as the sun we see,   14
    To rule the lightsome day:
       For certainly, &c.

15 But overwhelm'd and lost
  Was proud king Pharaoh
  With all his mighty host
  And chariots there also:
    For certainly, &c.

16 To him who pow'rfully
  His chosen people led,
  Ev'n through the desert dry,
  And in that place them fed:
    For certainly, &c.

17 To him great kings who smote·
    For his grace hath no bound.
18 Who slew, and spared not
  Kings famous and renown'd:
    For certainly, &c.

19 Sihon the Am'rites' king;
    For his grace lasteth ever:
20 Og also, who did reign
  The land of Bashan over:
    For certainly, &c.

21   Fo

22   :

mp 23

mf 24   :

∧

m 25

ff 26   :

p 1   wept,
              e thought on.
2 *In midst thereof we hang'd our harps*
  the willow-trees upon.

mp 3 For there a song required they,
 who did us captive bring:
m Our spoilers call'd for mirth, and said,
∧ A song of Sion sing.
p 4 *O how the Lord's song shall we sing*
 within a foreign land?
mf 5 If thee, Jerus'lem, I forget,
 skill part from my right hand.
 6 My tongue to my mouth's roof let cleave,
 if I do thee forget,
 Jerusalem, and thee above
 my chief joy do not set.
mp 7 Remember Edom's children, Lord,
 who in Jerus'lem's day
∧ Ev'n unto its foundation,
 Raze, raze it quite, did say.
mf 8 O daughter thou of Babylon,
 near to destruction;
 Bless'd shall he be that thee rewards,
 as thou to us hast done.
 9 Yea, happy surely shall he be
 thy tender little ones

∧ Who shall lay hold upon, and them
 shall dash against the stones.

mf 1

2
 toward thy sanctuary.
 I'll praise thy name, ev'n for thy truth,

3
 when I to thee did cry;
 And thou my fainting soul with strength

4

5

FOR GREAT'S THE GLORY OF THE LORD,
  WHO DOTH FOR EVER REIGN.

m 6 Though God be high, yet he respects
    all those that lowly be;
mf   Whereas the proud and lofty ones
    afar off knoweth he.

mp 7 Though I in midst of trouble walk
mf   I life from thee shall have:
    Gainst my foes' wrath thou'lt stretch
      thine hand;
    thy right hand shall me save.
  8 Surely that which concerneth me
    the Lord will perfect make:
    Lord, still thy mercy lasts; do not
    thine own hands' works forsake.

PSALM CXXXIX.
French 44.   Solomon 103.

m 1 O LORD, thou hast me search'd and
    known.
  2   Thou know'st my sitting down,
  And rising up; yea, all my thoughts
    afar to thee are known.

3   y always;

4

5

mp 6

m 7 From
    or fro
8

9

10

11

Then surely shall the very night
about me be as light.
12 Yea, darkness hideth not from thee
but night doth shine as day:
To thee the darkness and the light   *mp* 17
are both alike alway.

13 For thou possessed hast my reins,   *mf*
and thou hast cover'd me,
When I within my mother's womb   18
inclosed was by thee.
14 Thee will I praise; *for fearfully*
p   *and strangely made I am;*
m   Thy works are marv'llous, and right   *mp* 19
my soul doth know the same. [well   *m*

15 My substance was not hid from thee,   20
when as in secret I
Was made; and in earth's lowest parts   21
was wrought most curiously.
16 Thine eyes my substance did behold,
yet being unperfect;   can
And in the volume of thy book   *mf* 22 With
my members all were writ;   my

in number be:

mp 23 Search me, O God, and know my heart,
  try me, my thoughts unfold:
24 And see if any wicked way
  there be at all in me;
  And in thine everlasting way
  to me a leader be.

PSALM CXL.
Ballerma 114.   *Morven 99.*

mp 1 LORD, from the ill and froward man
  give me deliverance,
 And do thou safe preserve me from
  the man of violence:
2 Who in their heart mischievous things
  are meditating ever;
 And they for war assembled are
  continually together.
3 Much like unto a serpent's tongue
  their tongues they sharp do make;
 And underneath their lips there lies
  the poison of a snake.
4 Lord, keep me from the wicked's hands,
  from vi'lent men me save;

mf 7

10 Let burning coals upon them fall,
    them throw in fiery flame,
And in deep pits, that they no more
    may rise out of the same.

11 Let not an evil speaker be
    on earth established:
Mischief shall hunt the vi'lent man,
    till he be ruined.

mf 12 I know God will th' afflicted's cause
    maintain, and poor men's right.

13 Surely the just shall praise thy name;
    th' upright dwell in thy sight.

PSALM CXLI.
Crowle 153.   *St. Neot 150.*

mp 1 O LORD, I unto thee do cry,
    do thou make haste to me,
And give an ear unto my voice,
    when I cry unto thee.

m 2 As incense let my prayer be
    directed in thine eyes;
And the uplifting of my hands
    as th' ev'ning sacrifice.

3

4

T

:

p

· *our*

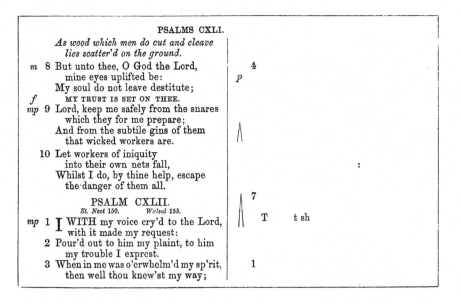

PSALMS CXLI.

As wood which men do cut and cleave
lies scatter'd on the ground.

m 8 But unto thee, O God the Lord,
  mine eyes uplifted be:
  My soul do not leave destitute;
f   MY TRUST IS SET ON THEE.
mp 9 Lord, keep me safely from the snares
  which they for me prepare;
  And from the subtile gins of them
  that wicked workers are.

 10 Let workers of iniquity
  into their own nets fall,
  Whilst I do, by thine help, escape
  the·danger of them all.

PSALM CXLII.
St. Neot 150. *Walsal 155.*

mp 1 I WITH my voice cry'd to the Lord,
  with it made my request:
 2 Pour'd out to him my plaint, to him
  my trouble I exprest.
 3 When in me was o'erwhelm'd my sp'rit,
  then well thou knew'st my way;

Give thou an answer unto me,
and in thy righteousness.

2 Thy servant also bring thou not
in judgment to be try'd:
Because no living man can be
in thy sight justify'd.

3 For th' en'my hath pursu'd my soul,
my life to ground down tread:
In darkness he hath made me dwell,
p   *as who have long been dead.*

4 *My sp'rit is therefore overwhelm'd*
in me perplexedly;
Within me is my very heart
amazed wondrously.

m 5 I call to mind the days of old,
to meditate I use
On all thy works; upon the deeds
I of thy hands do muse.

mf 6 My hands to thee I stretch; my soul
thirsts, as dry land, for thee.

7 Haste, Lord, to hear, my spirit fails:
hide not thy face from me;

m 8
mf
m

m 10

11

12

Another of the same.

Abbey Close 177. Old 143d 179.

mp 1 OH, hear my prayer, Lord,
    And unto my desire
    To bow thine ear accord,
    I humbly thee require;
    And, in thy faithfulness,
    Unto me answer make,
    And, in thy righteousness,
p   *Upon me pity take.*

mp 2 In judgment enter not
    With me thy servant poor;
    For why, this well I wot,
    No sinner can endure
    The sight of thee, O God:
    If thou his deeds shalt try,
    He dare make none abode
    Himself to justify.

  3 Behold, the cruel foe
    Me persecutes with spite,
    My soul to overthrow:
    Yea, he my life down quite

p *For, lo, my sp'rit doth fail:*
mp Hide not thy face in need;
    Lest I be like to those
    That do in darkness sit,
    Or him that downward goes
    Into the dreadful pit.

m 8 Because I trust in thee,
    O Lord, cause me to hear
    Thy loving-kindness free,
    When morning doth appear:
    Cause me to know the way
    Wherein my path should be;
    For why, my soul on high
    I do lift up to thee.

mp 9 From my fierce enemy
    In safety do me guide,
    Because I flee to thee,
    Lord, that thou may'st me hide.

m 10 My God alone art thou,
    Teach me thy righteousness:
    Thy Sp'rit's good, lead me to
    The land of uprightness.

p 4 *Man is like vanity; his days,*
   as shadows, pass away.

m 5 Lord, bow thy heav'ns, come down, touch
   the hills, and smoke shall they. [thou

6 Cast forth thy lightning, scatter them;
   thine arrows shoot, them rout.

7 Thine hand send from above, me save;
   from great depths draw me out;
   And from the hand of children strange,

8   Whose mouth speaks vanity;
   And their right hand is a right hand
   that works deceitfully.

mf 9 A new song I to thee will sing,
   Lord, on a psaltery;
   I on a ten-string'd instrument
   will praises sing to thee.

10 Ev'n he it is that unto kings
   salvation doth send;
   Who his own servant David doth
   from hurtful sword defend.

mp 11 O free me from strange children's hand,
   whose mouth speaks vanity;

And their right hand a right hand is
   that works deceitfully

m 12 That, as the plants, our sons may be
   in youth grown up that are;
   Our daughters like to corner-stones,
   carv'd like a palace fair

13 That to afford all kind of store
   our garners may be fill'd;
   That our sheep thousands, in our streets
   ten thousands they may yield.

14 That strong our oxen be for work,
   that no in-breaking be,
   Nor going out; and that our streets
   may from complaints be free.

mf 15 Those people blessed are who be
   In such a case as this;
   YEA, BLESSED ALL THOSE PEOPLE ARE,
   WHOSE GOD JEHOVAH IS.

PSALM CXLV.

Grafenberg 139.   *New Cambridge* 80.   *Old Glasgow* 121.

mf 1 I'LL thee extol, my God, O King;
   I'll bless thy name always.

2 Thee will I bless each day, and will
    thy name for ever praise.
3 Great is the Lord, much to be prais'd;
    his greatness search exceeds.
4 Race unto race shall praise thy works,
    and shew thy mighty deeds.

5 I of thy glorious majesty
    the honour will record;
  I'll speak of all thy mighty works,
    which wondrous are, O Lord.
6 Men of thine acts the might shall show,
mp   thine acts that dreadful are;
mf And I, thy glory to advance,
    thy greatness will declare.

7 The mem'ry of thy goodness great
    they largely shall express; [EXTOL
  WITH SONGS OF PRAISE THEY SHALL
    THY PERFECT RIGHTEOUSNESS.
m 8 The Lord is very gracious,
    in him compassions flow;
mp In mercy he is very great,
    and is to anger slow.

11

O

:

16 Thine hand thou open'st lib'rally,
    and of thy bounty gives
Enough to satisfy the need
    of ev'ry thing that lives.

mf

17 The Lord is just in all his ways,
    holy in his works all.
18 God's near to all that call on him,
    in truth that on him call.
19 He will accomplish the desire
    of those that do him fear:
He also will deliver them,
    and he their cry will hear.

20 The Lord preserves all who him love,
    that nought can them annoy:
p   *But he all those that wicked are*
    will utterly destroy.
f 21 MY MOUTH THE PRAISES OF THE LORD
    TO PUBLISH CEASE SHALL NEVER:
LET ALL FLESH BLESS HIS HOLY NAME
    FOR EVER AND FOR EVER.

And shall sing praises cheerfully,
Whilst they thy righteousness relate.

mp 8 The Lord our God is gracious,
Compassionate is he also·
In mercy he is plenteous,
But unto wrath and anger slow.

m 9 Good unto all men is the Lord:
O'er all his works his mercy is.

10 Thy works all praise to thee afford:
Thy saints, O Lord, thy name shall bless.

mf 11 The glory of thy kingdom show
Shall they, and of thy power tell:

12 That so men's sons his deeds may know,
His kingdom's grace that doth excel.

13 Thy kingdom hath none end at all,
It doth through ages all remain.

mp 14 The Lord upholdeth all that fall,
The cast-down raiseth up again.

m 15 The eyes of all things, Lord, attend,
And on thee wait that here do live,
And thou, in season due, dost send
Sufficient food them to relieve.

16

17

18

19

20

mp

f 21

FRAME
TO SPEAK THE PRAISES OF THE LORD:
TO MAGNIFY HIS HOLY NAME
FOR EVER LET ALL FLESH ACCORD.

PSALM CXLVI.

Saxony 102.   *Durham* 95.

f 1 PRAISE God. The Lord praise, O   *mp*
   my soul.

 2 I'll praise God while I live;
   While I have being, to my God
   in songs I'll praises give.

m 3 Trust not in princes, nor man's son,
   in whom there is no stay:

p 4 *His breath departs, to's earth he turns;*   *f* 10
   that day his thoughts decay.

mf 5 O happy is that man and blest,
   whom Jacob's God doth aid;
   Whose hope upon the Lord doth rest,
   and on his God is stay'd:

 6 Who made the earth and heavens high,   *mf*
   who made the swelling deep,
   And all that is within the same;
   who truth doth ever keep:

 7 Who righteous judgment executes   *m*
   for those oppress'd that be,

9

:

:

Who, while he gilds all na - ture's frame, Re - flects thy rays, and speaks thy name.

<table>
<tr><td colspan="2" align="center">PSALM</td></tr>
</table>

		That the dispers'd of Israel	
		doth gather into one.	
p	3	*Those that are broken in their heart,*	
		and grieved in their minds,	
mp		He healeth, and their painful wounds	*mf* 12
		he tenderly up-binds.	
m	4	He counts the number of the stars;	
		he names them ev'ry one. [POW'R;	
f	5	GREAT IS OUR LORD, AND OF GREAT	
		HIS WISDOM SEARCH CAN NONE.	
m	6	The Lord lifts up the meek; *and casts*	
p		*the wicked to the ground.* THANKS;	
f	7	SING TO THE LORD, AND GIVE HIM	
		ON HARP HIS PRAISES SOUND;	

His statutes and his judgments he
 gives Israel to know.
20 To any nation never he
 such favour did afford;
For they his judgments have not known.
f　　O DO YE PRAISE THE LORD.

PSALM CXLVIII.

St. Magnus 45.　　　*Old 29th 31.*

f 1 PRAISE God.　From heavens praise
 the Lord,
 in heights praise to him be.
2 All ye his angels, praise ye him;
 his hosts all, praise him ye.
3 O praise ye him, both sun and moon;
 praise him, all stars of light.
4 Ye heav'ns of heav'ns him praise, and
 above the heavens' height.　[floods

5 Let all the creatures praise the name
 of our almighty Lord:
For he commanded, and they were
 created by his word.

earth,

14 His people's horn, the praise of all
   his saints, exalteth he;
   Ev'n Isr'el's seed, a people near
   to him.   The Lord praise ye.

9

Another of the same.
Benedicite 183.   St. John 182.
f 1 THE Lord of heav'n confess,
        On high his glory raise.

10

   2 Him let all angels bless,
      Him all his armies praise.
   3   Him glorify

11

         Sun, moon, and stars;
   4   Ye higher spheres,

12

      And cloudy sky.

13

   5 From God your beings are,
      Him therefore famous make;
      You all created were,
      When he the word but spake.
   6   And from that place,
          Where fix'd you be
          By his decree,

14

          You cannot pass.

Ev'n those that be
Of Isr'el's race,
Near to his grace.
The Lord praise ye.

PSALM CXLIX.

St. Magnus 45.   *Colchester* 111.   *Hatzfield* 138.   *mf*

mf 1 PRAISE ye the Lord; unto him sing
a new song, and his praise
In the assembly of his saints   *a*
in sweet psalms do ye raise.   *mp* 7
2 Let Isr'el in his Maker joy,
and to him praises sing:
f   LET ALL THAT SION'S CHILDREN ARE
BE JOYFUL IN THEIR KING.   8

mf 3 O let them unto his great name
give praises in the dance·
LET THEM WITH TIMBREL AND WITH
HARP   9
IN SONGS HIS PRAISE ADVANCE.
mf 4 For God doth pleasure take in those   *mf*
that his own people be;

PSALM CL.

Chingford 91.   St. Magnus 45.

f 1 PRAISE ye the Lord.   God's praise
his sanctuary raise;   [within
And to him in the firmament
of his pow'r give ye praise.

mf 2 Because of all his mighty acts,
with praise him magnify:

ff   O praise him, as he doth excel
in glorious majesty.

with

4

:

END OF THE PSALMS.

TRANSLATIONS AND PARAPHRASES,

IN VERSE,

OF SEVERAL PASSAGES OF

SACRED SCRIPTURE.

I. GENESIS i.

St. Gregory 73.   Liverpool 69.

m 1 LET heav'n arise, let earth appear,
  said the Almighty Lord:
  The heav'n arose, the earth appear'd,
  at his creating word.

p 2 *Thick darkness brooded o'er the deep:*
f   God said, " LET THERE BE LIGHT:"
m   The light shone forth with smiling ray,
  and scatter'd ancient night.

 3 He bade the clouds ascend on high;
  the clouds ascend, and bear

6

He set the sun to rule the day,
  the moon to rule the night.

7 Next, from the deep, th' Almighty King
  did vital beings frame;
Fowls of the air of ev'ry wing,
  and fish of ev'ry name.

8 To all the various brutal tribes
  he gave their wondrous birth;
At once the lion and the worm
  sprung from the teeming earth.

9 Then, chief o'er all his works below,
  at last was Adam made;
His Maker's image bless'd his soul,
  and glory crown'd his head.

10 Fair in th' Almighty Maker's eye
  the whole creation stood.
He view'd the fabric he had rais'd;
  his word pronounc'd it good.

II. GENESIS xxviii. 20—22
Harrington 120.   *Dalkeith 85.*

mp 1 O GOD of Bethel! by whose hand

Who through this weary pilgrimage
  hast all our fathers led:

2 Our vows, our pray'rs, we now present
  before thy throne of grace:
m   God of our fathers! be the God
  of their succeeding race.

mp 3 Through each perplexing path of life
  our wand'ring footsteps guide;
Give us each day our daily bread,
  and raiment fit provide.

4 O spread thy cov'ring wings around,
  till all our wand'rings cease,
And at our Father's lov'd abode
  our souls arrive in peace.

m 5 Such blessings from thy gracious hand
  our humble pray'rs implore;
mf   And thou shalt be our chosen God,
  and portion evermore.

III. JOB i. 21.
St. Mary 145.   *Evan 125.*

mp 1 NAKED as from the earth we came,

Naked we to the earth return,
  and mix with kindred dust.
2 Whate'er we fondly call our own
  belongs to heav'n's great Lord;
The blessings lent us for a day
  are soon to be restor'd.

m 3 'Tis God that lifts our comforts high,
mp   or sinks them in the grave:
He gives; and, when he takes away,
  he takes but what he gave.
mf 4 Then, ever blessed be his name!
  his goodness swell'd our store;
His justice but resumes its own;
p   'tis ours still to adore.

IV.   JOB iii. 17—20.
St. Mary 145.   Evan 125.

p 1 HOW still and peaceful is the grave!
    where, life's vain tumults past,
Th' appointed house, by Heav'n's
  receives us all at last.   [decree,
2 The wicked there from troubling cease,
  their passions rage no more;

mp 1

the

2 As sparks in close succession rise,
    so man, the child of woe,
Is doom'd to endless cares and toils
    through all his life below.

3 But with my God I leave my cause;
    from him I seek relief;
To him, in confidence of pray'r,
    unbosom all my grief.

m 4 Unnumber'd are his wondrous works,
    unsearchable his ways;
  'Tis his the mourning soul to cheer,
    the bowed down to raise.

m 3

mp 5

VI. JOB viii. 11—22.
Morven 99.

m 1 THE rush may rise where waters
    and flags beside the stream; [flow,
mp But soon their verdure fades and dies
    before the scorching beam:

2 So is the sinner's hope cut off;
    or, if it transient rise,
'Tis like the spider's airy web,
    from ev'ry breath that flies.

m

VII. Job ix. 2—10.

St. Nicholas 151.

mp 1 HOW should the sons of Adam's race
　　be pure before their God?
　　If he contends in righteousness,
　　　we sink beneath his rod.

2 If he should mark my words and
　　with strict inquiring eyes, [thoughts
　Could I for one of thousand faults
　　the least excuse devise?

mf 3 Strong is his arm, his heart is wise;
　　who dares with him contend?
　Or who, that tries th' unequal strife,
　　shall prosper in the end?

4 He makes the mountains feel his
　　and their old seats forsake; [wrath,
　The trembling earth deserts her place,
　　and all her pillars shake.

5 He bids the sun forbear to rise;
　　th' obedient sun forbears:
　His hand with sackcloth spreads the
　　and seals up all the stars. [skies,

f 6 HE WALKS UPON THE RAGING SEA;
　　FLIES ON THE STORMY WIND:
p None can explore his wondrous way,
　　or his dark footsteps find.

VIII. Job xiv. 1—15.

Bangor 147.　　*St. Mary* 145.

mp 1 FEW are thy days, and full of woe,
　　O man, of woman born!
　Thy doom is written, "Dust thou art,
　　and shalt to dust return."

2 Behold the emblem of thy state
　　in flow'rs that bloom and die,
　Or in the shadow's fleeting form,
　　that mocks the gazer's eye.

3 Guilty and frail, how shalt thou stand
　　before thy sov'reign Lord?
　Can troubled and polluted springs
　　a hallow'd stream afford?

4 Determin'd are the days that fly
　　successive o'er thy head;
　The number'd hour is on the wing
　　that lays thee with the dead.

m 5 Great God! afflict not in thy wrath
　　　　the short allotted span,
　　　That bounds the few and weary days
　　　　of pilgrimage to man.

mp 6 All nature dies, and lives again:
　　　　the flow'r that paints the field,
　　　The trees that crown the mountain's
　　　　brow,
　　　and boughs and blossoms yield,

　7 Resign the honours of their form
　　　at Winter's stormy blast,
　　And leave the naked leafless plain
　　　a desolated waste.

m 8 Yet soon reviving plants and flow'rs
　　　anew shall deck the plain;
　　The woods shall hear the voice of
　　　Spring,
　　and flourish green again.

p 9 *But man forsakes this earthly scene,*
　　　ah! never to return:
　　Shall any foll'wing spring revive
　　　the ashes of the urn?

m 10 The mighty flood that rolls along
　　　　its torrents to the main,
　　　Can ne'er recall its waters lost
　　　　from that abyss again.

mp 11

pp 12

mp 13

m 14

IX. Job xxvi. 6, to the end.

Old 29th 31.   Now London 53.

m 1 WHO can resist th' **Almighty arm**
   that made the starry sky?
mp Or who elude the **certain glance**
   of God's all-seeing eye?
 2 From him no cov'ring **vails our crimes**;
   hell opens to his sight;
  And all Destruction's secret snares
   lie full disclos'd in light.

mf 3 Firm on the boundless void of space
   he pois'd the steady pole,
  And in the circle of his clouds
   bade secret waters roll.
 4 While nature's universal frame
   its Maker's pow'r reveals,
mp His throne, remote from mortal eyes,
   an awful cloud conceals.

mf 5 From where the rising day ascends,
   to where it sets in night,
  He compasses the floods with bounds,
   and checks their threat'ning might.

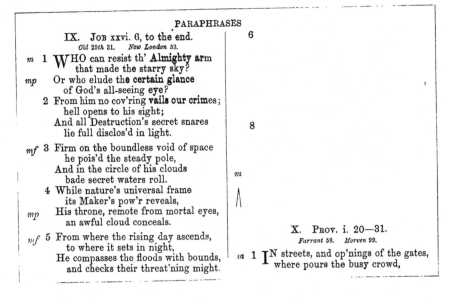

6

8

m

X. Prov. i. 20—31.

Farrant 58. Morven 99.

m 1 IN streets, and op'nings of the gates,
   where pours the busy crowd,

Thus heav'nly Wisdom lifts her voice, | *mp*
   and cries to men aloud:

2 How long, ye scorners of the truth, | ∧
   scornful will ye remain?
How long shall fools their folly love,
   and hear my words in vain?

3 O turn, at last, at my reproof!
   and, in that happy hour,
His bless'd effusions on your heart
   my Spirit down shall pour.

4 But since so long, with earnest voice, | *mf*
   to you in vain I call,
Since all my counsels and reproofs
   thus ineffectual fall;

p 5 *The time will come, when humbled low,*
   in Sorrow's evil day,
Your voice by anguish shall be taught,
   but taught too late, to pray.

f 6 WHEN, LIKE THE WHIRLWIND, O'ER THE | *m*
   COMES DESOLATION'S BLAST: [DEEP
mp   Pray'rs then extorted shall be vain, | ∧
p   *the hour of mercy past.* | V

m 5 According as her labours rise,
    so her rewards increase;
    Her ways are ways of pleasantness,   *mp*
    and all her paths are peace.

                                  m

XII. Prov. vi. 6—12.
Goldel 3.   *Evening Hymn* 187.

m 1 YE indolent and slothful! rise,
    View the ant's labours, and be wise;
    She has no guide to point her way,
    No ruler chiding her delay:
  2 Yet see with what incessant cares
    She for the winter's storm prepares;
    In summer she provides her meat,
    And harvest finds her store complete.

  3 But when will slothful man arise?
    How long shall sleep seal up his eyes?
    Sloth more indulgence still demands;
    Sloth shuts the eyes, and folds the hands.
  4 But mark the end; want shall assail,
    When all your strength and vigour fail;
    Want, like an armed man, shall rush
    The hoary head of age to crush.

6 With joy I saw th' abode prepar'd
　which men were soon to fill:
Them from the first of days I lov'd
　unchang'd, I love them still.

7 Now therefore hearken to my words,
　ye children, and be wise:
Happy the man that keeps my ways;
　the man that shuns them dies.

m 8 Where dubious paths perplex the mind,
　direction I afford;
Life shall be his that follows me,
　and favour from the Lord.

mp 9 But he who scorns my sacred laws
　shall deeply wound his heart,
He courts destruction who contemns
　the counsel I impart.

XIV. Eccles. vii. 2—6.
St. James 98.　　*Eversley 108.*

m 1 WHILE others crowd the house of
　and haunt the gaudy show, [mirth,
Let such as would with Wisdom dwell,
　frequent the house of woe.

2

and

4

m 2 Life is the season God hath giv'n
<   To fly from hell, and rise to heav'n;
mp That day of grace fleets fast away,
V   *And none its rapid course can stay.*

mp 3 The living know that they must die;
p   *But all the dead forgotten lie:*
  Their mem'ry and their name is gone,
  Alike unknowing and unknown.

mp 4 Their hatred and their love is lost,
  Their envy bury'd in the dust;
  They have no share in all that's done
  Beneath the circuit of the sun.

m 5 Then what thy thoughts design to do,
∧   Still let thy hands with might pursue;
V   Since no device nor work is found,
  Nor wisdom underneath the ground.

p 6 *In the cold grave, to which we haste,*
  There are no acts of pardon past:
  But fix'd the doom of all remains,
pp   *And everlasting silence reigns.*

m

p

V

m

voice

Men of Gomorrah! bend your ear
  submissive to his word.
2 'Tis thus he speaks: To what intent
  are your oblations vain?
Why load my altars with your gifts,
  polluted and profane?

3 Burnt-off'rings long may blaze to
  and incense cloud the skies; [heav'n,
The worship and the worshipper
  are hateful in my eyes.
4 Your rites, your fasts, your pray'rs, I
  and pomp of solemn days: [scorn,
I know your hearts are full of guile,
  and crooked are your ways.

5 But cleanse your hands, ye guilty race,
  and cease from deeds of sin;
Learn in your actions to be just,
  and pure in heart within.
6 Mock not my name with honours vain,
  but keep my holy laws;
Do justice to the friendless poor,
  and plead the widow's cause.

mf

3

mf 4

HIS SCEPTRE SHALL PROTECT THE JUST,
mp   and quell the sinner's pride.

m 5 No strife shall rage, nor hostile feuds
    disturb those peaceful years;
    To ploughshares men shall beat their
      swords,
    to prunning-hooks their spears.

6 No longer hosts encount'ring hosts
    shall crowds of slain deplore:
    They hang the trumpet in the hall,
    and study war no more.

mf 7 Come then, O house of Jacob! come
    to worship at his shrine;
    And, walking in the light of God,
    with holy beauties shine.

XIX. ISAIAH ix. 2—8.

Newington 63.   *Barrow 89.*

m 1 THE race that long in darkness piu'd
    have seen a glorious light;
    The people dwell in day, who dwelt
    in death's surrounding night.

XX. ISAIAH xxvi. 1—7.

St. Thomas 75.   *Tullis 93.*

m 6

mf 1 HOW glorious Sion's courts appear,
     the city of our God!
     HIS THRONE HE HATH ESTABLISH'D
     HERE FIX'D HIS LOV'D ABODE. [HERE,

mf 2 Its walls, defended by his grace,
     no pow'r shall e'er o'erthrow,
     SALVATION IS ITS BULWARK SURE
     AGAINST TH' ASSAILING FOE.

f 3 LIFT UP THE EVERLASTING GATES,
     THE DOORS WIDE OPEN FLING;
     ENTER, YE NATIONS, WHO OBEY
     THE STATUTES OF OUR KING.

m 1

     4 HERE SHALL YE TASTE UNMINGLED
mp   and dwell in perfect peace, [JOYS,
m   Ye, who have known JEHOVAH's
     and trusted in his grace. [name,

mf 5 Trust in the Lord, for ever trust,
     and banish all your fears;
     STRENGTH IN THE LORD JEHOVAH
     ETERNAL AS HIS YEARS. [DWELLS

mf 4 His dwelling, 'midst the strength of
    SHALL EVER STAND SECURE; [rocks,
    His Father will provide his bread,
    his water shall be sure.

mf 5 For him the kingdom of the just
    afar doth glorious shine;
    AND HE THE KING OF KINGS SHALL SEE
    IN MAJESTY DIVINE.

m 5

XXII. ISAIAH xl. 27, to the end.
St. Stephen 62.   New London 53.

mp 1 WHY pour'st thou forth thine anx-
    despairing of relief, [ious plaint,
    As if the Lord o'erlook'd thy cause,
    and did not heed thy grief?

2 Hast thou not known, hast thou not
    that firm remains on high [heard,
    The everlasting throne of Him
    who form'd the earth and sky?

m 8

m 3 Art thou afraid his pow'r shall fail
    when comes thy evil day?
    And can an all-creating arm
    grow weary or decay?

XXIII. Isaiah xlii. 1—13.

Ver. 1.5 Huddersfield 67.   St. Gregory 73.
Ver. 6-15 Vienna 40.   Sheffield 105.

m

m 1 BEHOLD my Servant! see him rise
        exalted in my might!
   Him have I chosen, and in him
   I place supreme delight.
   2 On him, in rich effusion pour'd,
      my Spirit shall descend;
   My truths and judgments he shall show
      to earth's remotest end.

mf 8

mp 3 Gentle and still shall be his voice
      no threats from him proceed;
   The smoking flax he shall not quench,
      nor break the bruised reed.
   < 4 The feeble spark to flames he'll raise;
   >   the weak will not despise;
   m   Judgment he shall bring forth to truth,
      and make the fallen rise.

f 9

mf 10

   5 The progress of his zeal and pow'r
      shall never know decline,

:

mf 11 Lo! former scenes, predicted once,
      conspicuous rise to view;
      And future scenes, predicted now,
      shall be accomplish'd too.
f 12 SING TO THE LORD IN JOYFUL STRAINS!
      LET EARTH HIS PRÁISE RESOUND,
      YE WHO UPON THE OCEAN DWELL,
      AND FILL THE ISLES AROUND!

                      m 2

  13 O CITY OF THE LORD! BEGIN
      THE UNIVERSAL SONG;
      AND LET THE SCATTER'D VILLAGES
      THE CHEERFUL NOTES PROLONG.   *mp* 3
m 14 Let Kedar's wilderness afar
      lift up its lonely voice;
      And let the tenants of the rock
      with accents rude rejoice;   4

f 15 TILL 'MIDST THE STREAMS OF DISTANT
      LANDS
      THE ISLANDS SOUND HIS PRAISE;
ff   AND ALL COMBIN'D, WITH ONE ACCORD,   *p* 5 *She may forget: nature may fail*
      JEHOVAH's GLORIES RAISE.   *a parent's heart to move;*

PARAPHRASES

mf   But Sion on my heart shall dwell
       in everlasting love.
6 Full in my sight, upon my hands
     I have engrav'd her name:
  My hands shall build her ruin'd walls,
     and raise her broken frame.

XXV. Isaiah liii.

Ver. 1-11 *St. Mary* 145.   *Silesia* 149.
Ver. 12-16 *New London* 53.   *Salisbury* 55.

mp 1 HOW few receive with cordial faith
     the tidings which we bring?
  How few have seen the arm reveal'd
    of heav'n's eternal King?
2 The Saviour comes! no outward pomp
    bespeaks his presence nigh;
  No earthly beauty shines in him
    to draw the carnal eye.

p 3 Fair as a beauteous tender flow'r
     amidst the desert grows,
  So slighted by a rebel race
    the heav'nly Saviour rose.

Mute, as the peaceful harmless lamb,
    when brought to shed its blood.

mp 10 Who can his generation tell?
    from prison see him led!
With impious show of law condemn'd,
    and number'd with the dead

11 'Midst sinners low in dust he lay;
    the rich a grave supply'd:
Unspotted was his blameless life;
    unstain'd by sin he dy'd.

m 12 Yet God shall raise his head on high,
    though thus he brought him low;
His sacred off'ring, when complete,
    shall terminate his woe.

13 For, saith the Lord, my pleasure then
    shall prosper in his hand;
His shall a num'rous offspring be,
    and still his honours stand.

14 His soul, rejoicing, shall behold
    the purchase of his pain;
And all the guilty whom he sav'd
    shall bless Messiah's reign.

15

mp
mf
mp 16

mf

mf 1

mp 2

mf 3

crowds repair?
gth

Incline your ear, and come to me;   *m* 9
the soul that hears shall live.
4 With you a cov'nant I will make,
that ever shall endure;
The hope which gladden'd David's   10
my mercy hath made sure.   [heart

5 Behold he comes! your leader comes,
with might and honour crown'd;
A witness who shall spread my name   11
to earth's remotest bound.
6 See! nations hasten to his call
from ev'ry distant shore;
Isles, yet unknown, shall bow to him   12
and Isr'el's God adore.

m 7 Seek ye the Lord while yet his ear
is open to your call;
While offer'd mercy still is near,
before his footstool fall.   *f* 13
8 Let sinners quit their evil ways,
their evil thoughts forego:
And God, when they to him return
returning grace will show.

m 14 Where briers grew 'midst barren
    shall firs and myrtles spring; [wilds,
    AND NATURE, THROUGH ITS UTMOST
    ETERNAL PRAISES SING.   [BOUNDS,

5

[find

...

XXVII. ISAIAH lvii. 15, 16.
French 44.   *Huddersfield* 67.

m 1 THUS speaks the high and lofty One;
    ye tribes of earth, give ear;
    The words of your Almighty King
    with sacred rev'rence hear:

  2 Amidst the majesty of heav'n
    my throne is fix'd on high;
    And through eternity I hear
    the praises of the sky:

  3 Yet, looking down, I visit oft
    the humble hallow'd cell;
    And with the penitent who mourn
    'tis my delight to dwell;

  4 The downcast spirit to revive,
    the sad in soul to cheer;
    And from the bed of dust the man
    of heart contrite to rear.

m 1

2

3

4

helple

y

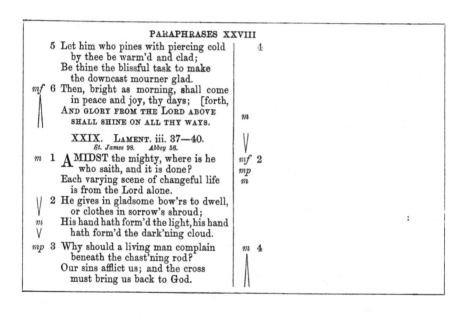

5 Let him who pines with piercing cold
   by thee be warm'd and clad;
Be thine the blissful task to make
   the downcast mourner glad.

mf 6 Then, bright as morning, shall come
   in peace and joy, thy days; [forth,
AND GLORY FROM THE LORD ABOVE
SHALL SHINE ON ALL THY WAYS.

XXIX. LAMENT. iii. 37—40.
St. James 98.   *Abbey* 56.

m 1 AMIDST the mighty, where is he
   who saith, and it is done?
Each varying scene of changeful life
   is from the Lord alone.

2 He gives in gladsome bow'rs to dwell,
   or clothes in sorrow's shroud;
m His hand hath form'd the light, his hand
   hath form'd the dark'ning cloud.

mp 3 Why should a living man complain
   beneath the chast'ning rod?
Our sins afflict us; and the cross
   must bring us back to God.

mp 5 As dew upon the tender herb,
diffusing fragrance round;

m As show'rs that usher in the spring,
and cheer the thirsty ground:

mf 6 So shall his presence bless our souls,
and shed a joyful light;
That hallow'd morn shall chase away
the sorrows of the night.

XXXI. Micah vi. 6—9.
St. Simon 43.   French 44.

mp 1 THUS speaks the heathen: How shall
the Pow'r Supreme adore? [man
With what accepted off'rings come
his mercy to implore?

m 2 Shall clouds of incense to the skies
with grateful odour speed?
Or victims from a thousand hills
upon the altar bleed?

3 Does justice nobler blood demand
to save the sinner's life?

p Shall, trembling, in his offspring's side
the father plunge the knife?

mf 4 No: God rejects the bloody rites
which blindfold zeal began;
His oracles of truth proclaim
the message brought to man.

m 5 He what is good hath clearly shown,
O favour'd race! to thee;
And what doth God require of those
who bend to him the knee?

6 Thy deeds, let sacred justice rule;
thy heart, let mercy fill;
And, walking humbly with thy God
to him resign thy will

XXXII. Habak. iii. 17, 18.
Canterbury 140.   Salisbury 55.

mp 1 WHAT though no flow'rs the fig-tree
clothe,
though vines their fruit deny
The labour of the olive fail,
and fields no meat supply?

2 Though from the fold, with sad sur-
prise,
my flock cut off I see;

Though famine pine in empty stalls,
  where herds were wont to be?

mf 3 Yet in the Lord will I be glad,
  and glory in his love;
In him I'll joy, who will the God
  of my salvation prove.

  4 He to my tardy feet shall lend
  the swiftness of the roe;
Till, rais'd on high, I safely dwell
  beyond the reach of woe.

  5 God is the treasure of my soul,
  the source of lasting joy;
A joy which want shall not impair,
  nor death itself destroy.

    XXXIII. MATTH. vi. 9—14.
    Martyrdom 64.   *Ballerma* 114.

m 1 FATHER of all! we bow to thee,
  who dwell'st in heav'n ador'd;
But present still through all thy works,
  the universal Lord.

  2 For ever hallow'd be thy name
  by all beneath the skies;

XXXIV. MATTH. xi. 25, to the end.   *mp* 6

Wiltshire 117.   *Comfort* 127.

m 1 THUS spoke the Saviour of the world,
    and rais'd his eyes to heav'n:
  To thee, O Father! Lord of all,   7
    eternal praise be giv'n.

m 2 Thou to the pure and lowly heart
    hast heav'nly truth reveal'd·
  Which from the self-conceited mind
    thy wisdom hath conceal'd.

  3 Ev'n so! thou, Father, hast ordain'd   *p* 1
    thy high decree to stand;
  Nor men nor angels may presume
    the reason to demand.

  4 Thou only know'st the Son: from thee   *m* 2
    my kingdom I receive;
  And none the Father know but they
    who in the Son believe.

mp 5 Come then to me, all ye who groan,   *mp* 3
    with guilt and fears opprest;
m   Resign to me the willing heart
    and I will give you rest.

4 Then in his hands the cup he rais'd,   3
  And God anew he thank'd and prais'd;
  While kindness in his bosom glow'd,
  And from his lips salvation flow'd:

m 5 My blood I thus pour forth, he cries,   4
  To cleanse the soul in sin that lies;
  In this the covenant is seal'd,
⋀ And Heav'n's eternal grace reveal'd.

6 With love to man this cup is fraught,   5
  Let all partake the sacred draught;
V Through latest ages let it pour,   ⋀
  In mem'ry of my dying hour.

XXXVI. Luke i. 46—56.
Arnold's 66.   St. Bernard 200.

m 1 MY soul and spirit, fill'd with joy,
    my God and Saviour praise,   *mp* 1
  Whose goodness did from poor estate
    his humble handmaid raise.

2 Me bless'd of God, the God of might, *m*
    all ages shall proclaim;   <
  From age to age his mercy lasts,   2
    and holy is his name.

mf Glad tidings of great joy I bring
    to you, and all mankind.

3 To you, in David's town, this day
    is born, of David's line,
  The Saviour, who is Christ the Lord;
m   and this shall be the sign:

4 The heav'nly Babe you there shall find
    to human view display'd,
mp All meanly wrapp'd in swaddling-
    and in a manger laid.   [bands,

m 5 Thus spake the seraph; and forthwith
    appear'd a shining throng
  Of angels, praising God; and thus
/\   address'd their joyful song:

f 6 ALL GLORY BE TO GOD ON HIGH,
    AND TO THE EARTH BE PEACE;
  GOOD-WILL IS SHOWN BY HEAV'N TO
  AND NEVER MORE SHALL CEASE. [MEN,

     XXXVIII.   LUKE ii. 25—33.
      St. Andrew 72.   *St. Thomas 75.*

m 1 JUST and devout old Simeon liv'd:
    to him it was reveal'd,

That Christ, the Lord, his eyes should
    ere death his eyelids seal'd.   [see

2 For this consoling gift of Heav'n
    to Isr'el's fallen state,
  From year to year, with patient hope
    the aged saint did wait.

3 Nor did he wait in vain; for, lo!
    revolving years brought round
  In season due, the happy day,
    which all his wishes crown'd.

4 When Jesus, to the temple brought
    by Mary's pious care,
  As Heav'n's appointed rites requir'd,
    to God was offer'd there,

5 Simeon into those sacred courts
    a heav'nly impulse drew;
  He saw the Virgin hold her Son,
    and straight his Lord he knew.

mf 6 With holy joy upon his face
    the good old father smil'd;
  Then fondly in his wither'd arms
    he clasp'd the promis'd child:

m 7 And while he held the heav'n-born
      Babe,
    ordain'd to bless mankind,
    Thus spoke, with earnest look, and
      heart
    exulting, yet resign'd:

mp 8 Now, Lord! according to thy word,
    let me in peace depart;
mf   Mine eyes have thy salvation seen,
    and gladness fills my heart.

9 At length my arms embrace my Lord,
    now let their vigour cease;
mf At last my eyes my Saviour see,
    now let them close in peace.

mf 10 This great salvation, long prepar'd,
    and now disclos'd to view,
    Hath prov'd thy love was constant still,
    and promises were true.

11 That Sun I now behold, whose light
    shall heathen darkness chase,
    And rays of brightest glory pour
    around thy chosen race.

XXXIX. Luke iv. 18, 19.
Old Glasgow 121.   *Chingford* 91.

mf 1 HARK, the glad sound, the Saviour
    the Saviour promis'd long; [comes!
    LET EV'RY HEART EXULT WITH JOY,
    AND EV'RY VOICE BE SONG!

m 2 On him the Spirit, largely shed,
    exerts its sacred fire;
    Wisdom and might, and zeal and love
    his holy breast inspire.

mf 3 He comes! the pris'ners to relieve,
    in Satan's bondage held;
f   THE GATES OF BRASS BEFORE HIM
    THE IRON FETTERS YIELD. [BURST,

mf 4 He comes! from dark'ning scales of
    to clear the inward sight; [vice
    And on the eye-balls of the blind
    to pour celestial light.

5 He comes! the broken hearts to bind
    the bleeding souls to cure;
    And with the treasures of his grace
    t' enrich the humble poor.

6 The sacred year has now revolv'd, *p*
  accepted of the Lord,
  When Heav'n's high promise is ful- *m* 4
  and Isr'el is restor'd. [fill'd,

f 7 OUR GLAD HOSANNAHS, PRINCE OF *mp*
     PEACE!
     THY WELCOME SHALL PROCLAIM; *m* 5
     AND HEAV'N'S EXALTED ARCHES RING
     WITH THY MOST HONOUR'D NAME. *mp*

XL. LUKE xv. 13—25. 6
Ballerma 114. *Martyrdom* 64.

mp 1 THE wretched prodigal behold
       in mis'ry lying low,
     Whom vice had sunk from high estate, *mf* 7
       and plung'd in want and woe.
m 2 While I, despis'd and scorn'd, he cries,
       starve in a foreign land,
     The meanest in my father's house 8
       is fed with bounteous hand:
     3 I'll go, and with a mourning voice <
       fall down before his face: <

9 Thus joy abounds in paradise
   among the hosts of heav'n,
Soon as the sinner quits his sins,
   repents, and is forgiv'n.

m

∧

mp

XLI. JOHN iii. 14—19.
Eatington 123.   *St. Stephen* 62.

m 1 AS when the Hebrew prophet rais'd
   the brazen serpent high,
The wounded look'd, and straight were
   the people ceas'd to die: [cur'd,

2 So from the Saviour on the cross
   a healing virtue flows;
Who looks to him with lively faith
   is sav'd from endless woes.

mp

∧

m 2

mp 3 For God gave up his Son to death,
m   so gen'rous was his love,
That all the faithful might enjoy
   eternal life above.

mp 4 Not to condemn the sons of men
   the Son of God appear'd;
No weapons in his hand are seen,
   nor voice of terror heard:

4 Thence shall I come, when ages close,   4
    to take you home with me;
There we shall meet to part no more,   wi
    and still together be.

5 I am the way, the truth, the life:
    no son of human race,
But such as I conduct and guide,   *mp* 1
    shall see my Father's face.

XLIII. JOHN xiv. 25—28.
Solomon 103.   *St. Mirren* 97.

p 1   *YOU now must hear my voice no more;*   *p* 2
    my Father calls me home;   *an*
m   But soon from heav'n the Holy Ghost,   *pp*
    your Comforter, shall come.

2 That heav'nly Teacher, sent from God,   *f.p* 3
    shall your whole soul inspire;
Your minds shall fill with sacred truth,
    your hearts with sacred fire.   <

mp 3 Peace is the gift I leave with you;   *f.p* 4
    my peace to you bequeath;   *m*
m   Peace that shall comfort you through   *f*
    and cheer your souls in death. [lifo,

f.m 5 'TIS FINISH'D—All his groans are past;
    his blood, his pain, and toils,
    Have fully vanquished our foes,   4
f   AND CROWN'D HIM WITH THEIR SPOILS.

f.m 6 'TIS FINISH'D—Legal worship ends,
    and gospel ages run;
f   ALL OLD THINGS NOW ARE PAST AWAY,   *mp* 5
    AND A NEW WORLD BEGUN.

XLV. ROMANS ii. 4—8.
Morven 99.   St. Chad 152.

mf 1 UNGRATEFUL sinners! whence
    this scorn
    of God's long-suff'ring grace?
    And whence this madness that insults
    th' Almighty to his face?

2 Is it because his patience waits,
    and pitying bowels move,
    You multiply transgressions more,
    and scorn his offer'd love?

3 Dost thou not know, self-blinded man!
    his goodness is design'd

mp 6

m 6

f C

mp

...

p *And, humbled low, confess their guilt*
    before heav'n's righteous Lord.

m 3 No hope can on the law be built
      of justifying grace;
      The law, that shows the sinner's guilt,
      condemns him to his face.

mf 4 Jesus! how glorious is thy grace!
      when in thy name we trust,
      Our faith receives a righteousness
      that makes the sinner just.

XLVII. ROMANS vi. 1—7.
St. Thomas 75.   Lancaster 68.

m 1 AND shall we then go on to sin,
      that grace may more abound?

mp Great God, forbid that such a thought
      should in our breast be found!

m 2 When to the sacred font we came,
      did not the rite proclaim,
      That, wash'd from sin, and all its stains,
      new creatures we became?

mp 3 With Christ the Lord we dy'd to sin;
mf   with him to life we rise,

is
m 4 Too
mf

...

mf 1

m 2
V
mf

3

f 4 WHERE IS THE JUDGE WHO CAN CON-
SINCE GOD HATH JUSTIFY'D? [DEMN,
WHO SHALL CHARGE THOSE WITH GUILT
OR CRIME
FOR WHOM THE SAVIOUR DY'D?

ff 5 THE SAVIOUR DY'D, BUT ROSE AGAIN
TRIUMPHANT FROM THE GRAVE;
AND PLEADS OUR CAUSE AT GOD'S
OMNIPOTENT TO SAVE. [RIGHT HAND,

mf 6 Who then can e'er divide us more
from Jesus and his love,
Or break the sacred chain that binds
the earth to heav'n above?

m 7 Let troubles rise, and terrors frown,
and days of darkness fall;
THROUGH HIM ALL DANGERS WE'LL
DEFY,
AND MORE THAN CONQUER ALL.

m 8 Nor death nor life, nor earth nor hell,
nor time's destroying sway,
Can e'er efface us from his heart,
or make his love decay.

m 9

...

m

2

:

Nay, gave my body to the flames,
  still fruitless were the deed.

mp 5 Love suffers long; love envies not;
    but love is ever kind;
    She never boasteth of herself,
    nor proudly lifts the mind.

m 6 Love harbours no suspicious thought,
    is patient to the bad;
    Griev'd when she hears of sins and
    and in the truth is glad.   [crimes,

7 Love no unseemly carriage shows,
    nor selfishly confin'd;
    She glows with social tenderness,
    and feels for all mankind.

8 Love beareth much, much she believes,
    and still she hopes the best;
mp   Love meekly suffers many a wrong,
    though sore with hardship press'd.

mf 9 Love still shall hold an endless reign
    in earth and heav'n above,
    When tongues shall cease, and prophets
    and ev'ry gift but love.   [fail,

m 10 Here all our gifts imperfect are;
    but better days draw nigh,
    When perfect light shall pour its rays,
    and all those shadows fly

m 11 Like children here we speak and think,
    amus'd with childish toys;
    But when our pow'rs their manhood
    reach,
    we'll scorn our present joys.

mp 12 Now dark and dim, as through a glass,
    are God and truth beheld;
mf   Then shall we see as face to face,
    and God shall be unvail'd.

13 Faith, Hope, and Love, now dwell on
    earth,
    and earth by them is blest;
    But Faith and Hope must yield to Love
    of all the graces best.

14 Hope shall to full fruition rise,
    and Faith be sight above:
    These are the means, but this the end;
    for saints for ever love.

L.   1 CORINTH. xv. 52, to the end.   *f*

Stroudwater 74   *St. Nicholas* 151.

p 1 *WHEN the last trumpet's awful voice*
         this rending earth shall shake,
      When op'ning graves shall yield their
      and dust to life awake;   [*charge,*

<

m 2 Those bodies that corrupted fell
            shall incorrupted **rise**,
         And mortal forms shall spring to life
            immortal in the skies.

                                              8

mf 3 Behold what heav'nly prophets sung
             is now at last fulfill'd,
          That Death should yield his ancient   *f*
             and, vanquish'd, quit the field. [reign,

f 4 LET FAITH EXALT HER JOYFUL VOICE,
            AND THUS BEGIN TO SING;

ff   O GRAVE! WHERE IS THY TRIUMPH NOW?
           AND WHERE, O DEATH! THY STING?   *p*

mp 5 Thy sting was sin, and conscious guilt,   *m*
             'twas this that arm'd thy dart;
          The law gave sin its strength and force
             to pierce the sinner's heart:

When once those prison-walls have   *m*
   by which 'tis now confin'd.   [fall'n

p 3 Hence, burden'd with a weight of clay,
    we groan beneath the load,
mp Waiting the hour which sets us free,
∧   and brings us home to God.
m 4 We know, that when the soul, un-
    shall from this body fly,   [cloth'd,
    'Twill animate a purer frame
    with life that cannot die.

   5 Such are the hopes that cheer the just;
    these hopes their God hath giv'n;
    His Spirit is the earnest now,
    and seals their souls for heav'n.
   6 We walk by faith of joys to come,
    faith grounded on his word;
∨ But while this body is our home,
    we mourn an absent Lord.

m 7 What faith rejoices to believe,
    we long and pant to see;
p   *We would be absent from the flesh,*
mf   and present, Lord! with thee.

mp 3 His greatness he for us abas'd,
    for us his glory vail'd;
    In human likeness dwelt on earth,
    his majesty conceal'd:
  4 Nor only as a man appears,
p   *but stoops a servant low;*
    Submits to death, nay, bears the cross,
    in all its shame and woe.

mf 5 Hence God this gen'rous love to men
    with honours just hath crown'd,
    And rais'd the name of Jesus far
    above all names renown'd:
m 6 That at this name, with sacred awe,
    each humble knee should bow,
    Of hosts immortal in the skies,
    and nations spread below:

mp 7 That all the prostrate pow'rs of hell
    might tremble at his word,
f   AND EV'RY TRIBE, and EV'RY TONGUE,
    CONFESS THAT HE IS LORD.

LIII. 1 THESSAL. iv. 13, to the end.
Comfort 127.   *Newington* 63.

mp 1 TAKE comfort, Christians, when your
    in Jesus fall asleep;   [friends
    Their better being never ends;
    why then dejected weep?
  2 Why inconsolable, as those
    to whom no hope is giv'n?
    Death is the messenger of peace,
    and calls the soul to heav'n.
  3 As Jesus dy'd, and rose again
mf   victorious from the dead;
    So his disciples rise, and reign
    with their triumphant Head.
  4 The time draws nigh, when from the
    clouds
    Christ shall with shouts descend,
f AND THE LAST TRUMPET'S AWFUL VOICE
    THE HEAV'NS AND EARTH SHALL
    REND.
m 5 Then they who live shall changed be,
    and they who sleep shall wake;

The graves shall yield their ancient
    charge,
and earth's foundations shake.
∧ 6 The saints of God, from death set free,
∧   with joy shall mount on high;
f   THE HEAV'NLY HOSTS WITH PRAISES
        SHALL MEET THEM IN THE SKY. [LOUD

mf 7 Together to their Father's house
        with joyful hearts they go;
∧   AND DWELL FOR EVER WITH THE LORD,
        BEYOND THE REACH OF WOE.
mp 8 A few short years of evil past,
m   we reach the happy shore,
∧   Where death-divided friends at last
        shall meet, to part no more.

LIV. 2 TIM. i. 12.
Gloucester 54.   Chichester 122.

m 1 I'M not asham'd to own my Lord,
        or to defend his cause,
    Maintain the glory of his cross,
        and honour all his laws.

∧ 2

p

∧
m

mf 3 Henceforth there is laid up for me
 a crown which cannot fade;
 The righteous Judge at that great day
 shall place it on my head.

m 4 Nor _{ha}t_h the Sov'reign Lord decreed
 this prize for me alone;
 But for all such as love like me
 th' appearance of his Son.

  5 From ev'ry snare and evil work
 his grace shall me defend,
 And to his heav'nly kingdom safe
 shall bring me in the end.

LVI. Titus iii. 3—9.
Jackson's 51. *French 44.*

mp 1 HOW wretched was our former state,
 when, slaves to Satan's sway,
 With hearts disorder'd and impure,
p *o'erwhelm'd in sin we lay!*

mf 2 But, O my soul! for ever praise,
 for ever love his name,

Who turn'd thee from the fatal paths
 of folly, sin, and shame.

m 3 Vain and presumptuous is the trust
 which in our works we place,
 Salvation from a higher source
 flows to the human race.

m 4 'Tis from the mercy of our God
 that all our hopes begin;
 His mercy sav'd our souls from death
 and wash'd our souls from sin.

m 5 His Spirit, through the Saviour shed,
 its sacred fire imparts,
 Refines our dross, and love divine
 rekindles in our hearts.

f 6 THENCE RAIS'D FROM DEATH, WE LIVE
 AND, JUSTIFY'D BY GRACE, [ANEW;
 WE HOPE IN GLORY TO APPEAR,
 AND SEE OUR FATHER'S FACE.

mf 7 Let all who hold this faith and hope
 in holy deeds abound;
 Thus faith approves itself sincere,
 by active virtue crown'd.

LVII. Heb. iv. 14, to the end.

Chichester 122. Comfort 127.

m 1 JESUS, the Son of God, who once
>   for us his life resign'd,
mf   Now lives in heav'n, our great High
    and never-dying friend.   [Priest,

m 2 Through life, through death, let us to
    with constancy adhere;   [him
⋀   Faith shall supply new strength, and
⋀   shall banish ev'ry fear.   [hope

m 3 To human weakness not severe
    is our High Priest above;
⋀   His heart o'erflows with tenderness,
⋁   his bowels melt with love.

mp 4 With sympathetic feelings touch'd,
    he knows our feeble frame;
  He knows what sore temptations are,
    for he has felt the same.

mf 5 But though he felt temptation's pow'r,
    unconquer'd he remain'd;
  Nor, 'midst the frailty of our frame,
    by sin was ever stain'd.

◊
mf

>

LVIII. *Another Version of the same Passage.*

Communion 10

m 1

mf

2 He who for men their surety stood,
p   *And pour'd on earth his precious blood,*
mf   Pursues in heav'n his mighty plan,
     The Saviour and the friend of man.

3 Though now ascended up on high,
p   *He bends on earth a brother's eye;*
m   Partaker of the human name,
p   *He knows the frailty of our frame.*
m 4 Our fellow-suff'rer yet retains
     A fellow-feeling of our pains;
     And still remembers in the skies
     His tears, his agonies, and cries.

m 5 In ev'ry pang that rends the heart,
     The Man of sorrows had a part;
     He sympathizes with our grief,
     And to the suff'rer sends relief.
mf 6 With boldness, therefore, at the throne,
     Let us make all our sorrows known;
     And ask the aids of heav'nly pow'r
     To help us in the evil hour.

LIX. Heb. xii. 1—13.

French 44.   *St. Simon 43.*

mf 1 BEHOLD what witnesses unseen
       encompass us around;
mp   Men, once like us, with suff'ring try'd,
f   BUT NOW WITH GLORY CROWN'D.
m 2 Let us, with zeal like theirs inspir'd,
       begin the Christian race,
     And, freed from each encumb'ring
       their holy footsteps trace. [weight,

mf 3 Behold a witness nobler still,
p   *who trode affliction's path,*
mf   Jesus, at once the finisher
       and author of our faith.
m 4 He for the joy before him set,
       so gen'rous was his love,
     Endur'd the cross, despis'd the shame,
<   and now he reigns above.

m 5 If he the scorn of wicked men
       with patience did sustain,
     Becomes it those for whom he dy'd
       to murmur or complain?

6 Have ye like him to blood, to death,
  the cause of truth maintain'd?
And is your heav'nly Father's voice   *mp* 12 A
  forgotten or disdain'd?

7 My son, saith he, with patient mind   *mf*
mp   endure the chast'ning rod;
  Believe, when by afflictions try'd,   13
<   that thou art lov'd by God.
m 8 His children thus most dear to him
  their heav'nly Father trains,
  Through all the hard experience led   ...
  of sorrows and of pains.

9 We know he owns us for his sons,   *m*   1   ;
  when we correction share;
Nor wander as a bastard race   ∧
  without our Father's care.
10 A father's voice with rev'rence we   *mf* 2
  on earth have often heard;
  The Father of our spirits now
  demands the same regard.

11 Parents may err; but he is wise   *mp* 3
  nor lifts the rod in vain;

That our weak hearts no more may
    stray,
    but keep thy precepts still;
4 That to perfection's sacred height
    we nearer still may rise,
    And all we think, and all we do,
    be pleasing in thine eyes.

LXI. 1 Pet. i. 3—5.

New London 53.   *Gloucester 54.*

mf 1 BLESS'D be the everlasting God,
    the Father of our Lord;
f BE HIS ABOUNDING MERCY PRAIS'D,
    HIS MAJESTY ADOR'D.
m 2 When from the dead he rais'd his Son,
    and call'd him to the sky,
    He gave our souls a lively hope
    that they should never die.

  3 To an inheritance divine
    he taught our hearts to rise;
    'Tis uncorrupted, undefil'd,
    unfading in the skies.

3

5 But when the sons of men began
   with one consent to stray,
  At Heav'n's command a deluge swept   *p* 11
   the godless race away.
6 A diff'rent fate is now prepar'd
   for nature's trembling frame;   *f*
f   SOON SHALL HER ORBS BE ALL ENWRAPT   12
   IN ONE DEVOURING FLAME.   *ff*

m 7 Reserv'd are sinners for the hour
   when to the gulf below,
  Arm'd with the hand of sov'reign pow'r,   *m* 13
   the Judge consigns his foe.
  8 Though now, ye just! the time appears   ghts to
   protracted, dark, unknown,   ; [guard,
  An hour, a day, a thousand years,   *p* 14 *Expecting calm th' appointed hour,*
   to heav'n's great Lord are one.   *when, Na   's conflict o'er*

  9 Still all may share his sov'reign grace,   *mf*
   in ev'ry change secure;
  The meek, the suppliant contrite race,
   shall find his mercy sure.   ...
10 The contrite race he counts his friends,   *Newington* 63.
   forbids the suppliant's fall;   *mf* 1 BEHOLD th' amazing gift of love
                                         the Father hath bestow'd

On us, the sinful sons of men,
 to call us sons of God!
mp 2 Conceal'd as yet this honour lies,
 by this dark world unknown,
A world that knew not when he came,
 ev'n God's eternal Son.

mf 3 High is the rank we now possess;
 BUT HIGHER WE SHALL RISE;
m Though what we shall hereafter be
 is hid from mortal eyes:
 4 Our souls, we know, when he appears,
 shall bear his image bright;
For all his glory, full disclos'd,
 shall open to our sight.

mf 5 A hope so great, and so divine,
 may trials well endure;
mp And purge the soul from sense and sin,
 as Christ himself is pure.

LXIV. REV. i. 5—9
St. Alphage 118. *Belgrave* 110.

mf 1 To him that lov'd the souls of men
 and wash'd us in his blood,

ff 3

p

f 4

mf

With vials full of odours rich,
  and harps of sweetest sound.

m 8

3 These odours are the pray'rs of saints,
  these sounds the hymns they raise;
God bends his ear to their requests,
  he loves to hear their praise.

4 Who shall the Father's record search,
  and hidden things reveal?
Behold the Son that record takes,
  and opens ev'ry seal!

mf 9

mf 5 Hark how th' adoring hosts above
  with songs surround the throne!

f TEN THOUSAND THOUSAND ARE THEIR
        TONGUES;
  BUT ALL THEIR HEARTS ARE ONE.

f 10

mp 6 Worthy the Lamb that dy'd, they cry,
  to be exalted thus;
ff WORTHY THE LAMB, LET US REPLY,
  FOR HE WAS SLAIN FOR US.

11

mf 7 To him be pow'r divine ascrib'd,
  and endless blessings paid;

LXVI. Rev. vii. 13, to the end.

St. Asaph 42.   *Renfrew 76.*

f 1 HOW BRIGHT THESE GLORIOUS
   SPIRITS SHINE!
m   whence all their white array?
   How came they to the blissful seats
   of everlasting day?

p 2 Lo! *these are they from suff'rings great,*
<   who came to realms of light,
m   And in the blood of Christ have wash'd
   those robes which shine so bright.

mf 3 Now, with triumphal palms, they stand
   before the throne on high,
   And serve the God they love, amidst
   the glories of the sky.

   4 His presence fills each heart with joy,
   tunes ev'ry mouth to sing:
   By day, by night, the sacred courts
   with glad hosannahs ring.

mp 5 Hunger and thirst are felt no more,
   nor suns with scorching ray;

mp

mf 2

f 3 ATTENDING ANGELS SHOUT FOR JOY,
    AND THE BRIGHT ARMIES SING;
m   Mortals! behold the sacred seat
    of your descending King!
  4 The God of glory down to men
    removes his bless'd abode;
    He dwells with men; his people they,
    and he his people's God.

mp 5 His gracious hand shall wipe the tears
p   *from ev'ry weeping eye:*
m   And pains and groans, and griefs and
    fears,
    AND DEATH ITSELF, SHALL DIE.
m 6 Behold, I change all human things!
    saith he, whose words are true;
    Lo! what was old is pass'd away,
    and all things are made new!

f 7 I AM THE FIRST, AND I THE LAST,
    THROUGH ENDLESS YEARS THE SAME;
    I AM, IS MY MEMORIAL STILL,
    AND MY ETERNAL NAME.

m 8 Ho, ye that thirst! to you my grace
    shall hidden streams disclose,
    And open full the sacred spring,
    whence life for ever flows.

mf 9 Bless'd is the man that overcomes;
    I'll own him for a son;
    A RICH INHERITANCE REWARDS
    THE CONQUESTS HE HATH WON.
mp 10 But bloody hands and hearts unclean,
    and all the lying race,
    The faithless, and the scoffing crew,
    who spurn at offer'd grace;

  11 They, seiz'd by justice, shall be doom'd
p   *in dark abyss to lie,*
    And in the fiery burning lake
    the second death shall die.
m 12 O may we stand before the Lamb,
    when earth and seas are fled,
    And hear the Judge pronounce our
    name,
    with blessings on our head!

HYMNS.

HYMN I.

Newington 63. *St. David* 48

m 1 WHEN all thy mercies, O my God!
            my rising soul surveys,
mf   Transported with the view, I'm lost
            in wonder, love, and praise.

     2 O how shall words, with equal warmth,
            the gratitude declare
         That glows within my ravish'd heart!
            but Thou canst read it there.

m 3 Thy Providence my life sustain'd,
            and all my wants redrest,
mp   When in the silent womb I lay,
            and hung upon the breast.

     4 To all my weak complaints and cries
            thy mercy lent an ear,

m 5

     6

  <

m

mp
  <

mp   And, when in sins and sorrows sunk.
<   reviv'd my soul with grace.

m 9 Thy bounteous hand with worldly bli...   *m*
    hath made my cup run o'er;
    And, in a kind and faithful friend,
    hath doubled all my store.

*mf*10 Ten thousand thousand precious gif:
    my daily thanks employ;
    Nor is the least a cheerful heart,   *f*
    that tastes these gifts with joy.

   11 Through ev'ry period of my life   *mp*
    thy goodness I'll proclaim;
    And after death, in distant worlds,
    resume the glorious theme.

*mp*12 When nature fails, and day and night   *m*
    divide thy works no more,
mf   My ever grateful heart, O Lord,   *mf*
    thy mercy shall adore.

f 13 THROUGH ALL ETERNITY TO THEE   *mp*
    A JOYFUL SONG I'LL RAISE;
    FOR, OH! ETERNITY'S TOO SHORT
    TO UTTER ALL THY PRAISE.

mf 6 In Reason's ear they all rejoice,   5
      And utter forth a glorious voice;
f   FOR EVER SINGING, AS THEY SHINE,
      "THE HAND THAT MADE US IS DIVINE."

HYMN III.
Crowle 153.   St. Neot. 150.

1 WHEN rising from the bed of death,
    o'erwhelm'd with guilt and fear,
  I see my Maker face to face,
    O how shall I appear!

2 If yet while pardon may be found,   *mf*
    and mercy may be sought,
  My heart with inward horror shrinks,
    and trembles at the thought;

3 When thou, O Lord! shalt stand dis-
    in majesty severe,   [clos'd
  And sit in judgment on my soul,
    O how shall I appear!

4 But thou hast told the troubled mind, *m* 3
    who doth her sins lament,
  That timely grief for errors past   *f*
    shall future woe prevent.

4 TO THY GREAT NAME, ALMIGHTY LORD!   *m*
    WE SACRED HONOURS PAY,
    AND LOUD HOSANNAHS SHALL PROCLAIM
    THE TRIUMPHS OF THE DAY.

5 SALVATION AND IMMORTAL PRAISE   *p*
    TO OUR VICTORIOUS KING!
ff   LET HEAV'N AND EARTH, AND ROCKS AND
    WITH GLAD HOSANNAHS RING. [SEAS,
mf 6 To Father, Son, and Holy Ghost,   4
mp   the God whom we adore,
f   BE GLORY, AS IT WAS, AND IS,   *m*
    AND SHALL BE EVERMORE.

HYMN V.

Soldau 4.   *Old Saxony* 28.

p 1 *THE hour of my departure's come;*   *m*
    I hear the voice that calls me home:
    At last, O Lord! let trouble cease,   *p*
    And let thy servant die in peace.

Single Chants.

TALLIS.

FARRANT.

No. 13.

ALCOCK.

No. 14.

PURCELL.

INDEX TO SUPPLEMENT.

Him glo-ri-fy Sun, moon, and stars; Ye high-er spheres, And cloud-y sky.

241. Walton. L.M.

BEETHOVEN.

The Lord is just in His ways all, And ho-ly in His

242. St. Minver. C.M.   A. GROSVENOR.

Be mer - ci - ful to me, O God; Thy mer - cy un - to me

Do thou ex - tend; be - cause my soul Doth put her trust in Thee.

244. Spohr. C.M.

From L. SPOHR.

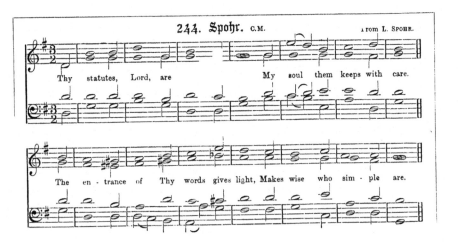

Thy statutes, Lord, are   My soul them keeps with care.

The en-trance of Thy words gives light, Makes wise who sim-ple are.

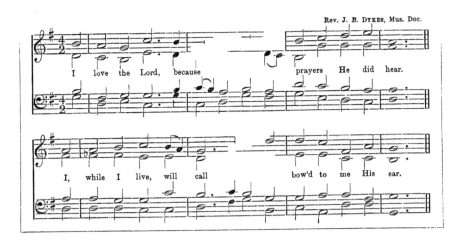

Rev. J. B. DYKES, Mus. Doc.

I love the Lord, because   prayers He did hear.

I, while I live, will call   bow'd to me His ear.

248. Dennis. S.M.

From NAGELI.

What man is he that fears The Lord, and doth Him serve?

Him shall he teach the way that he Shall choose, observe.

249. Franconia. S.M.

German Melody.
Har. from Rev. W. H. HAVERGAL

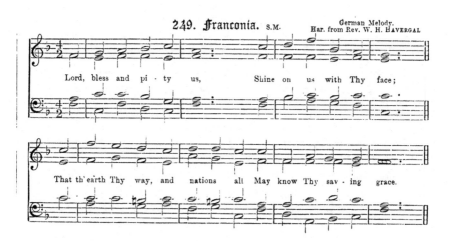

Lord, bless and pi - ty us, Shine on us with Thy face;

That th' earth Thy way, and nations all May know Thy sav - ing grace.

250. Zurich. S.M.

H. G. NAGELI.

What man is he that fears The Lord, and doth Him serve?

Him shall he teach the way that he Shall choose, and still ob - serve.

251. Cecilia. P.M.

Rev. L. G. Hayne.

Lo, I do stretch my hands To thee, my help a - lone.

For Thou well un - der - stands All

252. Milton. C.M.

From MASON'S *Hallelujah*.

Give ye the glo - ry to the Lord That to His name is due;

Come ye in - to His courts, and bring An of - fer - ing with you.

253. Bernard. C.M.

The *Merton Tune Book.*

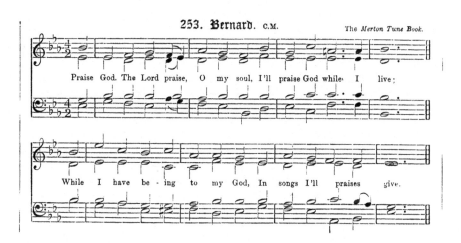

Praise God. The Lord praise, O my soul, I'll praise God while I live;

While I have be - ing to my God, In songs I'll praises give.

254. Palestrina. C.M.

From PALESTRINA.

Blessed are they that un de - fil'd, And straight are in the way;

Who in the Lord's most ho - ly law Do walk, and do not stray.

Lightning Source UK Ltd.
Milton Keynes UK
UKOW05f2201060617
302843UK00019B/1431/P